Angels in Disguise?

COMPILED AND EDITED BY
SUSAN CHEEVES KING

GRACE
Broken Arrow, OK

Royalties for this book are donated to World Christian Broadcasting.

Angels in Disguise?

ISBN-13: 978-1-60495-073-1

If you enjoyed

Short and Sweet's
The Kindness of Strangers

you might also enjoy
other books in the Short and Sweet Series

Short and Sweet
Small Words for Big Thoughts

Short and Sweet Too
More Small Words for Big Thoughts

The Short and Sweet of It
When the Right Word Is a Short Word

Short and Sweet Goes Fourth

Short and Sweet Takes the Fifth

Short and Sweet's
Family Album

Short and Sweet
A Different Beat

Short and Sweet's
Humili8ing
Tales We Wish Weren't True

Susan Cheeves King (p. 55) is the owner of Susan King Editorial Services: susankingedits.com. For over 24 years, Susan served with *The Upper Room* magazine. Currently she is continuing what she began in her role there as associate editor: speaking at Christian writers' conferences in the U.S. and Canada and editing and mentoring writers. Her professional life has also included teaching English and feature-writing classes at Lipscomb University, Biola University, and Abilene Christian University for a total of over 27 years.

Early in her career, she served as book editor and radio-program producer/on-air talent for The Institute of Scriptural Psychology, wrote magazine features as a freelance writer, and functioned as a seminar facilitator in leadership and group dynamics.

Susan and husband, Joe, live in middle Tennessee and have three grown children, two grandsons, and two foster grandsons.

Table of Contents

Introduction

I admit it. While I may be brave in mind, soul, and spirit; I'm not in body. So I think I must give off a damsel-in-distress vibe. Why else would I have experienced kindness from a stranger so often?

All my life, I have been blessed to work with Christians. But even when I'm out in the wide, wide world, I have met many more kind strangers than those of the other sort. And often this goes way past just being friendly or polite. At those times the stranger has had to give up something in order to be kind — to put his money where his mouth is, as it were. (See "Damsel in Distress" on page 55).

One of the most recent of these occurred at lunch with a friend. After she left to visit the ladies' room, a man about my age came up to tell me that he'd like to pay for my lunch. Even though I demurred more than once, he just said that he likes to help people. Later, I mused to my friend about why he would have done this. Did he hear me vent to her from his place at the next table? Or did I just look like a bag lady? (And what did other diners think when they saw him leave money by my plate?)

Especially in these trying times of pandemic and unrest, kindness from a stranger can change our view of the day or even our lives. Every time I run into a kind stranger, I think of him/her as an angel from God. And, in most cases, the stories in this book reveal the way God shows up in unexpected places and through unexpected people in our unpredictable world.

At various times in their lives, each of these writers has acted with great kindness — even toward strangers — so it was very challenging for them to switch their focus to what someone else has done for them.

Another challenge this book's authors faced was to write in a short-and-sweet style. This requirement conflicts with an attitude that all writers share. We love words. If a few words are good, many are better — especially the interesting word, maybe the elegant word . . . and definitely the special word only a particular writer can use. "This pen is being operated by a professional writer. Do not try this at home" is what we want to see at the bottom of every page we write.

But using the long, impressive words can work against good communication. The truth is, the best communication is what the readers/listeners understand with the least effort — a Mr. Spock mind meld as it were — as if the ideas are just flowing from the writer's mind to theirs with no actual words involved.

We may love words, but if we use too many of them and ones that are not familiar and comfortable to the average reader/listener, then words just get in the way. Writing tight (saying a lot with a little) and using crisp, clear, accessible words in our writing and speech bring joy to the readers/listeners even if they may not know exactly why.

So all of us — professionals and non-professionals alike — need to break our attachments to those polysyllabic aliens and get back to the simple words of our childhood. That's why this series was created. Like the others before it, Book 9 in the *Short and Sweet* series is based on an assignment I've been giving writers at conferences for over twenty years when I teach them about learning to write with excellent style: "Write about something close to your heart using words of only one syllable."

I allow the writers seven exceptions to the one-syllable-word-only requirement. Trust me; if you see a polysyllabic word in any of these stories, it is because that word fits into one of those exceptions.

If you're a writer — or aspire to be — and the challenge of writing in words of (mostly) one syllable intrigues you, why not give it a try? Contact me at shortandsweettoo@gmail.com to obtain the upcoming theme and deadline. You could be seeing your own work featured in the next book in the *Short and Sweet* series.

Susan Cheeves King

1

Surviving Bismo

by Mary Alice Archer

It was a thing of beauty, with its pink-and-white paint job and big black tires with white side walls. When I saw the 1956 Ford Ranch Wagon for sale in the lot, it was love at first sight. So in 1988 we bought this thirty-two-year-old car. It had a large V8 engine and big bench seats that made you feel as if you were on a nice couch. Also, the car had something called "Overdrive" that could be used to save gas on long trips along straight, flat roads.

On the other hand, with no seat belts, no air (A/C), a useless hand brake, a manual shifter on the steering column, and a very stiff clutch to step on, it was a bit of a challenge to drive. We named the car *Bismo* and loved it in spite of its flaws.

From our home in the mountains in Southern California, I drove my children to school every day over a steep and twisty road the width of barely two lanes.

One day on the way back home after dropping off the children, I drove Bismo around a bend on that road. On a downhill slope as I began to power up for a steep rise, I shifted into overdrive.

The gears jammed, and I found my car in neutral — and slowly rolling backwards down the two-lane road, with a hill on one side and an abrupt drop-off on the other.

I stepped hard on the brake but had to hold it down since the hand brake didn't work. So I was stuck on the hill as cars zipped around the curve and were forced to swerve into the other lane to avoid me.

Cell phones weren't here yet, but of course I had begun to pray.

Within minutes that felt like hours, a car drove toward me and stopped in its lane. One of the two young men in the car rolled down the window and asked, "What seems to be your problem?" When I sobbed out my plight, he jumped out of his car. "I bet I know what happened," he began. "I used to have a car just like this, and sometimes in overdrive the rods get tangled. I can fix that."

After he slid under the car, I heard some clinks and clacks, and then he slid back out with the words, "Now try putting it into gear."

It worked!

The young man zipped back into his car, and he and his friend drove off to my heart-felt cries of thanks.

I have no idea what my fate would have been if God hadn't sent those kind young men to me.

Were they angels in disguise? I say a big YES!

2

A Glimpse of a Husband's Love

by Toni Armstrong Sample

Dave lay in a bed in the ICU. I was told to call the children since his days would soon be over. I sat near his door in the hall, being of no use, for all I could do was wait. *Wait for what, the end, the kids, a miracle?* I could pray, but as I told our pastor, Chris, the only word that came to my mind was *help*.

"What does the word 'help' mean?" he said. "What do you ask of God with that word?"

My eyes were blank. "God knows."

"God knows?"

"Yes," I said. "God knows. The Holy Spirit knows. Jesus knows. His will be done; it will be done. He has a plan."

I can't recall if I had to squirm on a hard chair, but I did have to sit for hours while all I could do was wait and pray.

A nurse came through the door. Her badge read, "Jean." She had dark hair and a look of love in her eyes.

"Toni?" she asked.

"Yes," I was full of fear that she had come to tell me that Dave was gone.

"I want to tell you a story. May I?"

"Of course. About what?"

Nurse Jean began: "I met your David several weeks ago at Walmart. I was in the area where they sell books when I saw the lost look on his face. I told him who I was and asked if I could be of help to him." Jean stopped for breath, and I gave her a nod to go on.

"He told me his wife writes books. He was so proud of you. We stood there for ten minutes, and for ten minutes, I heard about this wife — source of his words and pride. He told me that you paint, make beads, and work with clay and that you met when you were a manager in a large company where you both worked. He said you were smart, beautiful, kind, and filled with love. In case you need to hear it again, he is so in love with you. I want you to know that, now, so that it will lift your spirits and give you strength for what is to come. It does not look good for Dave. He is at rest and in no pain. We can do no more than wait and see what his body does."

Tears ran from her eyes and also from mine. It was a strange time. A time when by her kind words, a woman I'd never met was able to fill me with joy not dread. Our hearts met that day, the hearts of two spirits who know the power of love — even between two strangers. She shared words that only she knew, and I will never let go of those words that came from Dave's heart. She gave me a view of who I was to Dave and what he felt and saw, and she gave me a glimpse of the depth of his love.

Had God caused that ICU nurse to be in the same place as Dave only weeks earlier?

I believe that Dave's words to Jean were his final gift to me, passed on by a nurse I'd never met and part of the perfect plan of the God I love.

3

My Super-Duper Uber Driver

by Terry Magness

I had never been to a convention of such size, nor in a place that big. It must have been three miles from one end of the hotel complex to the other, and we had to walk the full length and breadth many times over that week. I was also on my own in Orlando for the first time. Though among thousands of Christians, I had yet to see a face I knew. I felt alone.

On day two I awoke with a sinus infection. In years past, I had dealt with these often, but had learned how to avert them, at least, most of the time. But here in sunny Florida with all of its flowers, trees, and mold, I lost the fight. It was vital that I get on it right away with meds, or I would miss the rest of the event. I had seen a Walgreens just off the grounds, so I walked there.

I was shocked to learn that this "drugstore" had no pharmacy; the closest one that did was twelve miles away. With no other choice, I called in my order for that store, then walked back to the hotel. There, the concierge helped me load an Uber app on my phone and showed me how to use it. Deep inside, I wasn't at all sure how I felt about this whole Uber thing. Yet, since I had to pick up my meds, I used the app to book a ride.

The driver pulled up in front of the hotel, and still unsure, I got in the car and off we went. In no time at all, his warm and easy manner put my mind at rest. We talked the whole trip, as he shared about his family and job.

But when we pulled into Walgreen's lot, I learned my ride was booked only *one-way*.

"But you *will* take me back, won't you?"

"I am sorry, but you aren't booked, so they tell me I can't wait for you," he said sadly.

"But how will I get back to the hotel?"

He turned to face me in the back seat. "I will wait for you. Don't worry."

With that soft-but-firm pledge, he erased my fears.

I ran in to grab my order but had to wait in a line. When at last I got to the desk, the clerk told me my prescription was not there but had been filled at a *third* store many miles away. In a panic, I ran to tell my driver but met him at the end of the aisle.

"I'm sorry to tell you, I *must* leave." I told him about the mix-up and added, "They can fill the prescription here, but it will take a few minutes."

I could tell he really *had* to go but was torn as to what to do. I felt badly for him, yet I was truly in a fix. It seemed a long time when he at last took a deep breath and let his shoulders drop. The weight seemed to be gone, and I saw resolve in his eyes.

"Don't you worry about this. I will wait in the car, turn off the meter, and check out for the day. You take your time. Come to the car when you are through, and I'll take you back to your hotel."

His voice was as a father to his daughter. *Thank you, Lord.* I was not alone. When I came out of the store with my sack, I saw him there. True to his word, he drove me back to the hotel.

I don't know if Jesus has a place in this dear man's life, but I am sure that he was sent by my Father. He showered me with mercy, grace, and self-sacrifice in my hour — or two — of need. He will ever be my super-duper Uber driver.

4
A Child's Gift

by Susan Brehmer

Grandpa passed away. My brother and I had planned to see him soon but our visit came one week too late. We still made the trip and stopped at the house of a friend of my brother Steven on the way to see Grandma.

While at their house, I was given space to grieve.

A stream of tears ran down my face, only one sign of the raw place in my heart left open from the loss of my loved one.

Camped out on the floor alone, I had parked in front of the TV. An old film showed a scene of glad beach goers in the sun and sand, which clashed with my own gray, grief-filled mood.

With a far-off gaze, I sat lost in my thoughts and sad state. Close by, a young boy, the brother of Steven's friend, played with a cat and its young that bounced and moved about the room.

The child came over to where I grieved and held out a kitten to me. A new friend. A glimpse of soft warmth and joy. A gift that soon soothed the place where no words could come near.

When he saw my sad state, this boy who didn't know me had reached out in the best way he knew how — to show me a child's sense of love wrapped up in a sweet puff held out to me. All I had to do was reach for the gift.

When I looked at the gift in my lap, then up at the child who had shared from his heart, I was touched and just a bit less sad.

5

No Free Lunch?

by Alice H. Murray

On a nice October day, four of us sat at a table in a busy restaurant in Columbus, Georgia. The place was alive with the sound of the lunch crowd. All were there to eat, but we stood out from the rest. Our garb was not the same. Three of us wore our Sunday best. The man we were there to honor that day, my son-in-law, Joel, was clad in an Army dress uniform.

It was the best of times — a big day in Joel's military career. He had graduated from the Infantry Basic Officer Leader Course at Fort Benning. Every man in the class was older than him. To me, he seemed so young, but he was ready to lead men with guns. I couldn't have been more proud of Joel than if he had been my own son.

Next to Joel sat my daughter, Heather. She had a glow about her. Not only was she proud of her husband, but she was happy that she was going to be a first-time mom. She would give me my first grandchild. What a joy!

But it was also the worst of times. Now that Joel had graduated, he was being sent away for weeks to train in the field. He would not be home with his wife when she had need of him the most. Her pregnancy had not been an easy one; she had been in and out of the hospital. The two were new to the area, and my husband and I lived some four hours away. Heather and her new puppy would be on their own. What a time for Joel to be gone! Worry hung in the air, but we tried to focus on why we were with each other that day.

The food was tasty and soon eaten. With the end of the meal came the end of the happy time. It was now on to face the next step; Joel would have to get ready to leave. We sat and did not say a word as we kept a look out for the server to bring us the check. At last she came to our table, and Joel asked for the bill. With a big smile, she told him that it had been taken care of. Joel asked her who had paid for it. She told him that a diner had paid for the meal to thank him for his work for the USA.

I could see why a diner might want to treat my son-in-law to a meal. But this diner paid for *all* of our meals — Joel, his wife, and his in-laws as well. What a kind act! The diner must have known that a military job would be hard not only on the one in a uniform but his family as well.

I grew up in the South, and my mom taught me to thank a gift giver — in this case the gift of four meals. But I did not know whom to thank. So I did the first thing that came to my mind. After I got home, I wrote a note to the paper in Columbus, Georgia. I said that I had to let that nice diner know how much his or her kind act had meant to my family. I hope the diner saw what I wrote when it came out in print.

Some eight years later, I still think of this kind act and what it gave us. More than just a meal, that diner gave me the sense, deep in my heart, that people still act in kind and good ways to ones they don't even know. And I'm glad that my now-seven-year-old grandson can live in this better world.

In the best of times and the worst of times, I've even found a good reason to laugh from our meal out. When someone tells me there's no such thing as a free lunch, I have proof that they are wrong. On that day, my family got four of them!

6

Angels Change Tires

by Donna Miesbach

On a day with lots to do, I put my three small kids in the car and off we went. As I approached the 42nd Street exit, I heard a plane coming in low, as they had when we were at Ft. Dix, New Jersey. We learned to go out doors to get out of the way when the noise got to a peak. In fact, once on our way to the base we saw proof of a crash in the field near our home.

By now, the noise was quite loud, so I got out of the car to see where the plane was, but it wasn't a plane at all. It was my car. I had a flat tire! I had no idea tires could make that kind of noise, but I guess they do. I was in a fix, and I knew it. How could I hope to get my car fixed when help was a full three miles away? Back then, cell phones hadn't been thought of yet, so I was on my own — or so I thought.

It wasn't long before a car drove up and stopped. "Need some help?" called a voice full of cheer.

"I guess so! The tire is flat."

"No problem. I'll change it for you." Even though he was in a suit, he dropped to his knees and changed my tire.

"Oh no!" he said when I tried to pay him. "I just hope someone will stop and help my wife if she ever needs it." With that, he got in his car and pulled away.

I've heard that angels watch over us all the time. I don't know how true that is, but there is no doubt in my mind that I met one near the 42nd Street exit on that day so long ago.

7

A Hand Up from Many Hands

by Kenneth Avon White

It was a cool fall day in October when my plane touched ground at Washington, D.C.'s National Airport. Rhonda, my good friend from Houston, had taken time away from her Georgetown University study to pick me up in a taxi. She had begun her first year at Georgetown about six weeks prior.

As for me — after a year of gypsy life in California, I was back in Texas and on the ropes. I had no home to speak of. All of $75 had to stretch until the next Hail Mary. And no, there was no kin with a keen "call" to help. So Rhonda called me to Washington.

Like a mother hen who broods over her eggs until they've hatched, Rhonda began to hatch a plan to break me from my dark shell. In the cab, Rhonda pressed a sheet of paper into the palm of my hand. "Now here's the deal" she said in a tone sober at its core but laced with wonder. "You're gonna serve food at El Torito. I've set it up with the man in charge. I called him on my first day of class. Here's your pen. Here's the job app. Get busy." I thought for just a bit. I stared at the paper. "It's going to be just fine," Rhonda cooed. Then a switch in tone. "Get at it!"

In just a few, I was face-to-face with the El Torito boss. My Texas roots and love of its real Mexican food paid off. Once I poured out the finer points of the enchilada, chalupa, and quesadilla, I was given a start date and thrown a crisp black apron.

For the next three weeks Rhonda's dorm room would be my

home — a home filled with kind strangers. Enter Fiona — the first young lady to stretch out a kind hand of help. With grace, Fiona made it known that I was in a safe place — this was quite the stretch since she and Rhonda knew that their offer broke school rules into bits. Fiona was a rich kid sent to study law and she shared loads of plush bed spreads, sheets and quilts with me to make my nights on the floor warm and free of bruised ribs.

I soon met Stacey from New Jersey. She was an Italian siren with a firm frame and short, jet-black hair like that of Zelda Fitzgerald and F. Scott's jazz age friends. Then there was Ramona from Westchester County, Connecticut — a Sarah Lawrence grad. Her face was rosy, her hair a stream of blonde curls, and her slim fingers just built for the arts. They were the part of Rhonda's "A" team that helped keep me fed on my day's off from El Torito where I got a free lunch on work days.

Stacey was a bit bold. Under her coat, she would sneak both meat and a side dish or two from the dorm cafe. Ramona was more of an under-the-radar girl. Sweets and snacks were tucked into her small Gucci purse to keep me going.

If I were to live there; I would need to brush teeth, bathe, and take "bio breaks" — no small feat in a girl's dorm. That's where two more strangers, Christine and Brittany, came in. Their room was down the hall next to the loo (as our British friends call it). Each dawn, Christine clocked in to walk me down, check to make sure the coast was clear, and stand guard at the door as I groomed for the day. Brittany took on the bio breaks for the rest of the day and into the night. It was her job to clear the deck and shoo away those who tried to enter when I just *had* to go. Christine, with her jolly laugh and silly self, took it all in stride. Brittany, with poise and a more legal view of things, had to act quite out of her orbit, which made her help all the more prized.

Yes, we had our share of close calls. Still, in spite of antic after antic and caper after caper, these elite of Georgetown University would work as a team each day to fill the needs of a guy who was down on his luck. To them it was a hand up, not a hand out.

This went on for three weeks until I had enough money to rent a room on my own.

I write this in a time of COVID-19. When I see on the news the long food lines, the bright signs on home doors that say, "time to move on" and those with only change to their names, I can relate to a bit of that. I, too, was once in dire need of the basics of life and did not know where to turn. I think there's no time like now to "pay it forward" — to take a page out of the book of these women who knew me not but chose to pick me up and help plant my feet on solid ground.

8

She Gave Me Hope

by Shelley Pierce

Our daughter's first sign of what was to come showed up when she was in fifth grade. Her first kidney stone was followed by more than we could count. But kidney stones weren't her only pain. Auto-immune illness can strike at any time in life. Our daughter's fight began just before high school. As her list of symptoms grew, doctors didn't know what to do with her. We seemed to go from one hospital to the next to no avail.

As I sat next to her bed in a new hospital, miles from home, I cried out to God, "Where are you, Lord?"

After hours of pain, she finally fell into a deep sleep. My heart was heavy. My head ached. The worry was almost more than I could bear.

I took a deep breath and made up my mind to find the cafeteria while she slept. This hospital was like a small city. The trip piled upon my raw nerves.

Alone in the elevator, eyes cast down, I began the ride to the right floor.

The elevator stopped and a woman strode in.

But this ride, with a guest I didn't know, was not like any other.

She set her gaze on mine and spoke. "I know you're feeling hopeless, but don't lose heart. God hears your prayers, and answers will come. Keep believing."

The doors opened, and she left me in my thoughts. Her words had taken my heavy heart and given it peace. I looked up as if God was afloat in the elevator and told Him thank you for the woman I didn't know who spoke the right words, ones that soothed my heart.

Answers didn't come at that time; the road ahead was long.

But since then, our daughter and her husband have been graced by the birth of a sweet baby girl. A long-hoped-for miracle of life.

I will never forget the lady I did not know who spoke hope to me when I needed it most.

9

The Flirt

by Wilma Vernich

Rain and hail beat down on the hood of my truck as I peered through the blur at the road in front of me. My right foot switched back and forth from the gas to the brake as cars slowed to yet one more stop. I thought I had planned my trip well, but this storm was not part of that plan. At this rate, it looked more and more as if I would be late to my job interview.

And then . . .

The low-on-gas light blinked on.

Oh, no! my brain screamed. In a flash, I saw in my mind's eye the debit card still at home . . . on the desk . . . and not with me. To add to my upset, I had no cash with me. Now I was miles from home with the gas gauge on "E" and I was too late and too far from home to turn back.

But, I did have checks.

I took a quick glance at the clock on the dash and made what I hoped was a good choice. I zipped in at the first sign that read "Gas" and hopped out of the truck into the rain. I prayed the store clerk would give me some grace, take my check, and send me on my way so I could snag that job.

Nope.

My nice work suit, my best smile, and my sweet pleas for help fell on deaf ears and a hard heart.

"We take cash and card only — absolutely no personal checks," the clerk said in a cold voice, with a firm shake of her head. "You can try down the street. Maybe they can help you."

Fine, I thought. *Why waste my time to duke it out with a fence post?*

At the next place, I had to go to the end of a long line that snaked to the clerk. But she did look as if she might be nice. I heaved a big sigh as a man in his late 60s got in line to wait with me.

"You sure look pretty today, ma'am!" His whole face beamed.

"Thank you," I said through clinched teeth. *Great. Now on top of everything else, I have to wait in this long line with a flirt standing behind me.*

I began to shift from foot to foot with the silly thought that it might help speed up the line and get me out of there. But the clock ticked on.

At last it was my turn with the clerk.

I spilled my guts to Clerk #2 who at least heard me out to the end of my whole tale of woe. But she, too, said she could not take my check. Her boss would not let her.

To make my last point, I laid out all the change I had culled from each nook and niche of my truck — a whole 89 cents.

I begged.

I moaned.

I groaned.

I begged some more.

Clerk #2 looked me in the eye and said, "I'm sorry."

I then spoke to her in my calm voice, "What am I supposed to do now? In less than twenty minutes, I have a job interview." Could she not see this by my heels and pearls? "I have no gas to get there or get home afterward because I left my debit card at home. All I need is just . . . five . . . dollars . . . of . . . gas. Can I *puh-lease* write you a small check for just five dollars so I can buy enough to get me to my interview on time? If need be, hold my check; and I'll come back later with the cash!"

Clerk #2 called her boss to the front of the store. He said his store's rule still stood.

Just then a kind voice in back of me spoke up.

"Here, Miss. Is this enough? I turned to see "the flirt" pull a $20 bill from his coat and hand it to the clerk. "I'll buy her gas," he said.

I was floored. I had no words. I felt small. I tried to write him a check.

"Just pay it forward," my new friend said with a wink, "and good luck with that job interview."

By the skin of my teeth, I did make it to my interview. I did not get the job. But — more than once — I have paid it forward.

10
Delivering Before Delivery

by Beth Brubaker

It was a hot day in July, and I had to go to the store. It wasn't my choice to be out. With no car, the trip to the store would be a long walk with one small child in a stroller and one still tucked inside me for the next two months. To top it off, I had to lug a cart with me! So I got creative and strapped the cart loose to my waist with bungee cords. It took a while to find the right length of cord so the cart wouldn't hit my legs, but I did it. I tried but couldn't work it so that the cart grip wouldn't bounce off my rear with every step. I'm sure I made quite a sight, not only going to the store but also going down the aisles as I shopped.

Look out for the Mom Train. *Toot, toot!*

My quest for food over; I checked out, put my bags in the cart, fixed my cords, and set off to trudge home in the heat.

I made it to the store lot when a man saw me and my odd, rigged train and asked if he could help by taking my bags home for me. I was wary at first, but he swore my food would be home when I got there. I said yes and gave him my address. I prayed that I had made the right choice.

The walk home was fast but full of hope that he not only dropped my food at home, but that he had dropped them off at the right spot. I lived on the first floor of a duplex, but the front door was shared and on the side of the house.

At first when I turned onto my block, I saw no bags on my stoop. My heart jumped until I moved close to see a flash of white and brown. All my bags were lined up next to my door, close to a bush so no one could see them from the street. A small note was tacked onto one of the bags.

You don't know me, but I was glad to help. Have a great day and drink water!

His note made me smile. I took my son and the bags inside, got us both a nice, long drink of water, and put my feet up.

I never saw that kind man again, though his deed is in my heart for life.

11

Raining Kindness

by Valerie Runyan

Although we'd had a good time with our family that Mother's Day, we faced a long drive home. My husband, Norman, and I were both tired but glad that we met very few cars on the road. It was near dark as cold winds blew and dark clouds loomed above us. Then as slow drops of rain turned into fast sheets of sleet . . . *bang*! I thought we had hit a rock, a *big* rock from the sound of it. As we were to learn later, our SUV had "hydroplaned." It spun to our left and then turned over onto the driver's side as we slid across the lanes! Only by the grace of God were no cars or such in the lanes as we spun off the road and then surged more yards until we hit mounds of dirt.

When we came to a stop, I hung in mid-air over Norman! The air bags on all sides of us had burst open. We both spoke. I was fine, but Norman had many pains. Since he was pinned into a small space, I could not reach to help. I fought hard to move through the tight space I was in. Then I found the strap to press my seat belt and pushed it. With that I was freed . . . and fell down on top of Norman. He was glad but hurt, so he made jokes like, "Just give me more warning so I can get out of the way." We laughed at how we must look — that is until he found that his ribs hurt when he laughed.

As I crawled through the seats to get to the back, I saw through the glass many cars and SUV's stopped, and some were there to help us! At that point, I saw that our SUV was ripped wide open at the back, the only place I could find to crawl out. Norman, though, was trapped and in pain. Two women helped me up the hill as a group of men began to work to get my husband out. Wet sleet hit my face. The wind was so cold! When we reached the top, a teen girl held a car's door open for me. As I slid in, I saw an older teen, her brother, in the back. He gave me a small smile as I sat down. Their mother, the driver, said that she was glad I'd not been hurt. I thanked them for a place to just sit and warm up. After a time, I asked if I could use a cell phone to call our family.

The mother drove some yards one way up the road and then back the other way to try to pick up a signal. When she did, I called both of our sons. I was not yet able to give them any news about their dad but told them we would be in touch. I gave back the cell and thanked God for those He had put in our path.

As we sat in the car, the teens talked about how they liked school and did well. The boy spoke of what he hoped to do that summer. Then he spoke in low tones of his plans to go to the Air Force Academy in Colorado. We shared brief thoughts about the day's end, Mother's Day, and more. All the while I looked down the hill with my focus on my husband and what was taking so long.

Then at one point a man came up to the car. He told me my husband was in a lot of pain. That put a cold shot of fear in me. But he also said a call had been made to bring help. He walked back down the hill. I stared as he dropped out of sight.

In the car, what had been a good chat shut down. It was still and quiet as I stared out of the car, my eyes ever fixed on the scene down the hill. As I began to break down, I felt an arm slip over my back as the teen boy moved near me. What he did renewed my calm and strength. He kept his arm there until help drove up. Then I thanked this fine and caring family and bade them well.

Norman recovered. He and I are sure that God placed all those folks by our side that cold night in May.

12

Happy All the Day

by Cynthia Conner Goyang

1966

On a warm June day, I make my way down the block and back round the way to that happy place. I begin to mount four white steps to a cute two-story church. Shyly, I tap at the door. No reply. I feel mixed up. I tap again. "Hmm," I frown and back away slow, sad. As I turn to leave, the door opens. I turn back. I'm all of five years old. I can't hide the joy in my eyes. The lady, still in her robe, stands with a sweet smile that tugs at her lips. "Hi little one. Cynthia . . . is it? Are you here for Sunday Night Service?"

I can only nod shyly. The only other time I've been here was a few weeks back.

"You're an hour early, sweet girl," she says.

I turn once again to leave. Sad.

"Cynthia?" The pastor's wife calls, "Come on in, baby girl."

Timid, I turn with a happy heart and trail after her up to the second floor. She seats me at a small table. Then she goes to the fridge. She comes back with apple juice and yummy food. "There you go, dear. I'm going to go get ready for our church service, okay?" She taps the tip of my nose. "You wait right there, and we'll come and get you in just a bit, okay?"

My tummy growls, the sound so loud I think she must have heard. My five-year-old eyes tear. Today is one of the many times that the fridge at my house is bare. I sit, quiet, and eat. I enjoy every bit. More than that — I love the quiet talk back and forth, back and forth, of the pastor and his wife.

No yells, nor rants, no hits, no chaos.

In this house, at the age of five, I see the hands and feet and love of God alive.

In just a bit, the pastor and his wife come in — ready in suit and a fine dress. Their nice scent fills the air. With great love, they greet me. How can they hold so high a young child who can't even tell time yet? With God's love, they speak kind words to me then hold my hands and lead me down the stairs. They seat me in the very front row.

Soon after, others come in. We sing songs to the Lord. We adore Him who came to save those high and those all of five years old, like me.

We sing . . . I sing:

> *At the cross, at the cross where I first saw the light,*
> *And the burden of my heart rolled away*
> *It was there by faith I received my sight,*
> *And now I am happy all the day!*

The small kind acts of that pastor and his wife showed me an image of a happy home — full of Christ's love, peace, and joy. Since then, I have come to know Christ — His love, His peace, His joy . . . and that I can be:

"Happy all the day."

"At the Cross" (*"Alas, and Did My Savior Bleed?"*) lyrics by Isaac Watts (1674-1748)

Beyond the Call of Duty

by Deb Johnston

When a loved one is ill, the world can feel like a place that holds no warmth or no close bonds. Due to COVID-19, I am the sole guest, the only one who can be at the hospital bed by my husband's side. At one point the doctors talk about an air lift to a unit in Madison two hours from us, but this day we meet a new helper as Nurse Heather starts to work on my spouse's case. She checks on him often. She knows the pain he is in and keeps in touch with his doctors. She is the wave of pure light we learn about in high school labs. Behind the scenes, she emits this beam in high form toward the needs of my spouse.

Heather is clear and spot on. When the surgeon stops in to tell me what will come next Nurse Heather says, "I'm here, I'll listen with you. I'll help you remember."

As the doctor tells me all the side effects, Nurse Heather looks me in the eye and soothes me with, "We got this." In some rare way, she lends her strength to me. Later I am told that my husband will go to the OR in less than an hour. "Let's get you set," Heather says. "You need to text your sons so they can get here as soon as they are able."

Life can change at the speed of light. I sit down next to my loved one's bed — pinned there by this heavy load. I think about all the "what ifs," but those "what ifs" only block me from that first step that will lead me to the next one.

In a very deep way, Heather's calm lifts me up and makes me sure that I am not alone. That's when I say a prayer of thanks for the gift of a stranger on this day. A gift that fills me with peace.

14

A Small Act
with a Long Shelf Life

by Frank Caudle

So it goes every day. (Isn't that the way of a habit?) For me, it's my java juice, my A.M. call. Maybe it's the kick. But it could be the taste. I don't know what it is, but it's real to me. It calls me. It needs me, or do I need it? Your guess. I still don't know.

At my local WAWA store, the bean juice is self-serve. Do your own thing. Mine is with two creams. I say I'm so sweet I don't need sugar. After I put the lid on, I head to the front of the store to stand in line. While I wait, I start small talk with the man in front of me — such a nice man and of a race not my own. Let me say it again, *nice* man. The line is slow, but in front of us it starts to get short. The talk goes on. At the other end, the line starts to get long.

At last, we are at the front of the line. When he goes to buy his cuppa joe, he buys my mine, too. I say no, but he doesn't heed what I say. That's the man in him. He has a hard head. But his is a nice kind of hard head.

I thank him, and side by side we walk toward the door. That's where the talk turns to Jesus. He goes to church every Sunday. So do I. Nice man. Real man. Godly man.

I ask where his church is. He says about ten miles away. I plan to visit him there but as of yet, I have not. Shame on me.

Though some may call it a small thing, what he did when he bought my brew left a stamp on me that has stuck in my mind to this day. We did not know each other, and I have not seen him since. Yet it was as if this man wrote the book about what it means to treat a stranger like a friend, to be nice with no hope to get paid back. Being nice is right, at all times. His kind act reminds all of us to do the same.

I still don't know his name, but that day he was my model of Mark 9:41: *"Whoever gives you a cup of water in My name, because you belong to Christ, assuredly, I say to you, he will by no means lose his reward"* (NKJV).

This man showed me that to give was a way of life for him. That is how I know that one day, when we are both with Jesus, this man will have an extra star in his crown for all to see.

The Wind I Did Not See

by S.E. Pruitt

I live in Salinas, California, and we can get high winds. One day, I parked near the National Steinbeck Center and swung open the door of my Nissan. Just then, it was torn out of my hand by a gale-force wind that had warmed only about one degree since it left the North Pole. The door hit and then scraped the right side of the car in the next space.

Of course, the car was white. No way could anyone miss the four-inch-wide swath of Persian blue paint on its side. Worse, the mark was at least a foot long.

Sick with guilt, my mind rang with thoughts of a law suit, insurance rates, and the car owner's rage. In truth, my first thought was to close my car door and drive home, but my parents, bands of Sunday school teachers, and the Bible have made it quite clear to me that I can't hide from God.

I am not a brave person. Doing the right thing would turn me to jelly. I walked into the Steinbeck Center with my insurance card in one sweat-damped hand and my now too-warm coat in the other. With each step, I prayed the car's owner would be calm. I prayed that if that hope was too much to ask for, at least he or she would not yell, or worse, sue me.

A half hour and many people later, I slunk into the museum's cafe where I had been told the car's owner worked.

The young woman was calm but grave as we walked out to look at the scrape. She eyed it for a long moment, then grinned and said, "Oh, don't worry! My husband can buff that out."

I am sure I looked scared because she added. "You poor thing. You must have been so worried. Come back inside."

A few minutes later, I was eating a free piece of carrot cake. "To settle your nerves" she said.

The cafe is long gone, but the kindness of one of its workers lives on. Her choice to smile and go easy on me turned a bad day into one of grace — and even cake.

It also taught me a truth. I have trouble forgiving. Stirred by her example, I know it is time to let go of old hurts.

I pray Matthew 5:7 for her: *Blessed are the merciful, for they shall receive mercy.* May God bless her life, and may all she meets be as kind to her as she was to me.

This memory clings to my mind the way her carrot cake sticks to my hips.

Launched by Compassion

by Desiree Glass

My husband was drunk again, but this time hell-bent on taking the boat out, and our seven-year-old son with him.

"No, you're not!" I cried. "You're drunk! And it's late. Timmy has school in the morn—" He scorned what I said and they left.

This time he had gone too far. I had to guard my son. I scooped up our daughter, only three, and drove to the dock.

When I got there, I saw my husband as he tried to launch the boat. It wouldn't steer right. He had to pull it out of the water. When he saw me, his anger flared. He rushed to my car and raised its hood to yank out the spark plugs. Then he got in his truck and sped off with the spark plugs — and our son.

My heart beat fast, and I began to shake. *What am I going to do?* It was dark, and my young daughter and I were stuck at a boat dock. I saw no one near to help, and I had no phone. Scared and hurt, I prayed and cried — and cried some more.

In time, other boats came to shore. My sobs were heard. A man and a woman came to my side and asked what was wrong. Once I began to talk, it all spilled out. The pain of years of abuse. They told me that I should leave him. The man took the spark plugs from their car and put them in mine.

"Do you have a place to go?" he asked.

"Yes, my mom and dad's. Thank you for all you did. You have been so kind," I said as I wiped my eyes.

As I turned the key to start the car and drive away, my thoughts were set on how to start a new life.

Strangers When We Met

by Jenny Calvert

I played the piano for a large adult choir of older-aged men and women fitly named Silvertones. Each week we met to learn the notes and words of our music, and then twice a month we would strut our stuff in schools and old-folk homes. I was new to the group as we had moved to Texas from Missouri only a few months prior. I was also the only young one in the choir.

One day a lady from the choir came to me and said, "Jenny, I know you're traveling to Missouri for your mom and dad's fiftieth anniversary. I want to take you shopping to buy a new dress." My jaw dropped. No friend or family had ever made an offer like that, and this was someone I'd just met.

Helen, a lady also in the choir, stood near us and heard these words. She saw my face and said, "Don't worry, Jenny. She does this all the time."

But no one had done this for me, and I was shocked.

The day to shop came, and a short while prior, the lady called to say, "Jenny, I want you to bring your children with you because I also want to buy them new outfits for the anniversary." I was thrilled that she thought of my kids. So I packed up the three of my five kids who still lived at home — Danny, Sarah, and Jonathan — and off we drove to the store. Once there, we split up to shop in the right place for our needs: Danny to the teen boys, Sarah to the girls, Jonathan to the boys, and me to the women's department. Our new clothes would be a dress for Sarah and for me, and nice shirt and pair of pants for both of the boys.

This lady did not know that our family was broke in dire need of help. We had moved to Texas for a better job for my husband. We didn't own any clothes that would be right for this event; and this lady, still alien to me, was going to dress all of us up to look nice. In our new duds, we would be able to hold our heads high at my parent's fiftieth-anniversary party.

I tried on many things and hung them up on two hooks, a "no" hook, and a "yes" hook, so that I could choose. In the end, my "yes" hook was full. I was stumped as I thought, *Okay, which one looks best? Which one should I get?* My kids had picked out their clothes, also. The choir lady floored me when she said, "I will buy all of them!"

"What?" I asked, in awe. "Are you kidding me? These racks are full, even the kid's racks. It's way too many! It will cost too much. You can't buy all of them."

"Yes, I can, and I will," she said, her face stern. "I want to do this. Do not argue with me." Her tone and her face told me that I had better not cross her. If she wished to bless us, no one else could vote pro or con. We were all quite stunned at this giant favor she'd heaped on us.

I did not know, at this time, but this lady, named Berniece, would go on to bless my family and me many times over. As I came to know her more, we found out that we were akin in many ways; one case in point was that we were both from Missouri. We liked many of the same things. We would laugh and cry as one. It didn't take long until Berniece would be more than a best friend. She would be the one to hear me, hold me, cheer me, and teach me. At times, she would scold me as if I were her daughter.

In fact, when we would have lunch dates, people would often say, "Are you and your mother having a girls' day out?" "Yes!" we would say with wink and a smile at each other. After all, not only did we look alike, but Berniece was like a mom to me. I would call her my "Texas Mom," and she would refer to me as her daughter. I loved her, and she loved me through and through.

Berniece is now with the Lord, and oh how I miss her! Yet I have been so blessed. I can look back in my mind and feel her soft hand in mine. I can see her big smile, and I can hear her voice as she laughs, sings, yaks, and blurts out funny quips. In my mind, I can see that great love she had for me as it shone from her eyes. Yes, God gave me a prize. It was not just gifts of clothes, food, cash, and school items for my kids. He gave me the gift of Himself — in a dear friend and saint named Berniece.

18

A Brick in the Road

by Penny L. Hunt

My exit was in sight, but coming at me in the other lane was a large truck — and in my lane, a brick. I hit the brick, which left a hole the size of the Grand Canyon in my right-front tire.

My car on shreds with sparks of metal, I pulled off the road. Then I limped to the front of a mini mart and went in to ask for help. All I got was a sneer, a curt response of, "No phone — no rest room," and the back of the clerk's head.

For years, my husband would pack the car and join me on trips to Christian women's clubs where I told the story of my life before Christ, how I met Christ, and what my life has been like since. But the day came when he couldn't go with me. I was on my own to pack — and had left without my purse.

Now, I was stuck at a mini mart with no cash, cards, ID, or cell phone. I would be late and had only a vague idea of how to change a tire. With no help in sight, I dug my way to the spare and had grabbed hold of the tire iron when a man in a Jeep drove up.

"Do you need help? I saw your boxes and thought you were in sales. Then I saw your tire."

I held tight to the iron. "No. Those are just props and books. I had to put them there so I could get the spare out and change the tire."

"You know how to do that?"

"Of course."

"Well, let me give you a hand."

I was kind. I let him change the tire. As he did, he asked where

I was going. I told him and he said, "No, you're not. Not on this tire. The road you have to take is up steep hills with miles of sharp twists and turns."

"Oh, I'll go slow. I'll be fine."

He shook his head. "There's a used tire shop just up the road. You can buy a tire there."

I bit my lip. "I can't. I don't have any money with me, and I left my purse at home," I blurt.

He wiped his hands on the front of his jeans. "I know I don't look like it right now," he said as he stretched to stand tall, "but I'm a very rich man. I own all the Aaron's Rent-to-Own stores in this area, and I'd like to buy you a tire. I don't have time to go with you and don't have much cash on me, but this should take care of it," he said and pressed two twenty-dollar bills in my hand.

The men at the tire shop were at the ready and could have put a NASCAR pit crew to shame in the time it took them to get that new tire on.

"How much do I owe you?" I asked the boss.

"All taken care of," he said. The man who called said to say, "Just pass it on."

I made the trip in time to speak. In that talk, I shared what my life was like before I met Christ, how I came to know Him, how He'd seen me through good times and bad, and that God makes a way where there is no way — and, just that day, had sent help to deal with a brick in the road.

Fear not, for I am with you; be not dismayed, for I am your God;

I will strengthen you,

I will help you,

I will uphold you with my righteous right hand.

Isaiah 41:10 ESV

Unable to Repay

by Janice Hagood LeMaster

Just as I was about to sit down from my day's work, the phone rang. The voice on the other end told me that Rob, one of my three sons, had been taken to the hospital. I grabbed my keys, ran out the door, and drove to the other side of town. As I made my way to the ER, I prayed non-stop.

At that time my Rob was thirty-eight years old. His job is to drive a large truck each day as he makes stops to drop freight on his route. He had paused to unload on the dock at one of his last stops when he fell to the ground. I was later told that my son could not reply or react at all. Someone who was there called for help. This is the stranger whose kindness changed my life.

A phone call does not seem to be a big event. After all, it doesn't take much work or seem an act that could save a life. But more often than we think, it takes a hero to be ready and able to call for help as the first step in a series of events.

Rob had a heart attack, which meant that EMTs were vital to save his life. They gave care that began the fight to keep him alive as he rode in an EMS van to the ER. He stayed in the ICU for six days as the staff kept up the work to help him reach the point that he could go home. He is now doing well and is back on the job. But if that call had not been made, those people would not have been able to save his life.

Even before he came home from the hospital, I began my work to try and find the one who'd made that call. First, I called the place where his trial began. No one seemed to know what I was talking about.

After Rob came home, I still tried to find the one who had made that vital call. Again — this time at a site that was close by — no one seemed to know what I meant. I even tried the fire house from which I thought the EMTs might have been sent.

I could not find any clue that would lead me to the one I yearned to reach.

We were able to thank all those who cared for him in the hospital but not the one who made my son's life begin anew as he went home to heal. Even though the trail has grown cold, I have not given up in my quest to find that kind stranger. Until then, I thank God for making those prayers for Rob come true.

Kindness Found

by Xavia Arndt Sheffield

I was in such a hurry to buy the few items left on my party list that I didn't even take my large purse, but just grabbed the small coin purse from it. As I dashed up and down the aisles, it sat in the top of my cart, and I did not give it a second thought. I should have, since once in a food store my purse was swiped from the top of my cart, and ever since, I had not put my purse in the top of a cart again. I had even warned more than one woman not to leave her purse in the top of the cart while she turned away to shop.

With all of my items in tow; I rushed through the line, paid my bill, and ran out. When I was half way home, I missed my purse. Haste had caused me to leave it in the top of my cart at the store. I sped back, madly searched the rows of carts, and asked at the desk if it had been found. The reply was no. I broke the speed limit on the way home and, in tears, told my husband. He began to call the bank cards to tell them of the loss.

Fifteen to twenty minutes later, I saw a strange car pull up to our house. My heart raced at the thought that the purse had been found. I didn't even wait for the car to come to a full stop but flew out of the house as fast as I could. A lady rolled down the side door glass, held up the purse, and asked me if it was mine. I told her yes! She and her husband had found it, looked into it to find out where I lived, and taken the time to drive all the way to my house to bring it to me.

At a loss for words, I gave each of them a big hug and held that purse to my heart as if it were of more value than a pile of gems. What shone clear and bright on that day though, was not a ruby but a kindness to me from two saints I had never met. Even though they acted as if it was just all in a day's work, the smiles on their faces told me that they were as happy about their good deed as I was. That day I learned to put some brakes on my rapid pace and focus more on the task at hand; but when I don't, I will thank God for the kind and honest ones among us.

21

Two Strangers in Hollywood

by Dennis Conrad

HOLLYWOOD, CALIFORNIA, 1969

As my high-school friends and I walked along Hollywood Boulevard to Grauman's Chinese Theater, we came upon a group. One stranger reached out and gave me a small book, *Have You Heard of the Four Spiritual Laws?* I tucked it in my suit-coat pocket.

As we passed the same group on our way back, another person held out a tract. I said, "No thank you" and kept on my way.

In an alcove, a dark-haired man in dirty clothes, who sat on the ground with his back to a gray metal door, looked at me and said, "Rot in hell."

I grew up in church, was baptized, and took a course in world religions. I did not want to rot in hell, so later that night I read the tract. My life did not change.

WHITTIER, CALIFORNIA, 1989

With high hopes, I drove over an hour to be with a woman for our second date. I made it my focus to get to know Diane from the first time I met her at Rio Hondo Community College. At her place, she had the idea that we each take our own car to the diner.

We liked our meal at Jack's Salad Bowl and got to know each other. I shared about my degree in Religious Studies with a focus on faith in Asia. As our meal ended, she stood up, gave me a small book, and excused herself to go to the restroom. "Maybe you would like to read this."

After I watched her walk away, I looked down at my hand to see *Have You Heard of the Four Spiritual Laws?*

Oh no, I thought. *This is the "rot-in-hell" book. I've got to read this.*

In one part, the book said "all have sinned and fall short of the glory of God." That is when all my faults were clear to me. At school I had made up my own religion. Later, I divorced my first wife, had many jobs and lady friends, danced at a Hare Krishna temple, and chanted Buddhist chants. I needed a fresh start. I thought that this might be my last chance.

I read all the way to the end of this short piece and then thought about the contents. When several minutes later Diane came back to our table, she asked, "What do you think of the booklet?"

"I prayed the prayer."

"You what?"

"I prayed the prayer. It's the one near the back."

We talked for a few minutes, and then I walked her to her car. We agreed to a third date, and then we drove away.

That night I went home, cleaned my apartment, and threw out things that made me think of my past. The next Sunday, I went to church with Diane.

Within eight months, Diane and I wed.

I stand in awe of God's ways. In 1969, two strangers in Hollywood helped me put my life in order and showed me kindness. It may have taken me twenty years to be ready to change, but it came about from when I met those men. And I give thanks for them both: the one who gave me the small Gospel book and also the one who said those harsh words. The first obeyed God when he was led to share the Good News on Hollywood Boulevard. As for what I would say to the second — *"You meant evil against me, but God meant it for good"* (Genesis 50:20 ESV).

Surrounded by Kindness

by Donna Morse

Crash! Jolt! The crunch, smash, and twist of car parts shook my whole body.

Oh no! I thought, as I viewed the wreck on that slick, rain-soaked street. Now I could not drive my car at all. The good thing was that no one was hurt. I sent up praise to God for that.

I felt so bad that the crash had been my fault. But the young man whose car I hit looked at me with kind eyes. "Things like this happen for a reason," he said. "We just have to accept them." I sensed no anger in his words or tone. Even though his car had borne the brunt of the crash, he brought a sense of calm to the scene.

A second man rushed over to view my car, which was stuck in the road with rush-hour traffic soon to start. "I'll help you get your car off the road," he said. He dropped to his knees in the rain to jack up the wheel and turn it so the car could move. Then he pushed it out of the road. His kind act helped to lift the worry I'd felt.

Soon a cop came to size up the scene. As he gave me my slip of shame, he said, "Don't be too hard on yourself. This is a very common thing."

When I heard his words, I didn't feel quite so dumb.

"Thank you," I said, stunned that even the long arm of the law had shown me mercy.

The last kind act came when a woman came out of the 7-11 store and walked across its lot where my car sat.

"Are you okay?" she asked.

"Yes," I assured her.

"You look so cold. I have tea for you." With a smile she held out a cup to me. "It should warm you up," she said with a quick nod.

"Thank you," I said. "That's very kind."

Then with a smile and one more nod, she left — but not before I caught a glimpse of the cross she wore. *Is this dear lady a sister in Christ?*

This scene had not been fraught with the anger and stress that a crash usually caused. Not groans, but grace was brought by this small group of strangers as each gave me a kind act in my time of need and shame. I asked the Lord to bless each one of these dear souls — all gifts from Him.

I hope that the next time someone causes me a trial due to their error, I too, will show mercy and a kind spirit.

A Dog's Day Out

by Nancy Brashear

Mommy! I want *her*!" Seven-year-old Christopher points at the thin, yellow mutt, who cries at the back of the cage she shares with a Rottweiler mix named Killer.

Killer barks, growls, drools, and bangs on the wire fence to let us know he is in charge.

The man who works at the dog pound taps his foot. "Look, here, lady. Make up your mind. We're about to close. You come back in the morning, she won't be here. See that date?" He points to a card taped to the gate. "Expired. Gone! Caput!"

Nine-year-old Pam cries out, "Mom! We need to save her!"

I turn to my three kids. "Will you take care of her? Feed her? Brush her? Take her on walks? Vote now!"

Pam, Chris, and Kelly raise their hands.

"It's a deal," I tell the man.

Shasta slinks her way to our car. Once in, she shrinks down flat on the floor by five-year-old Kelly's feet for the trip home.

We take Shasta to her new bed in the garage, and she rests from her day. Over the next week, she finds her place in our family and hearts. We learn that she doesn't even know her name.

A week later after the kids leave for school, I move her to her house out back before I head for work. I look up at gray clouds while a brisk breeze whips through the air.

At noon, the phone on my desk rings.

"I have a dog here. Shasta," a soft voice says. "Are you her human?"

Shasta? How'd she get out of our yard? My heart pounds at the thought of her loose on the street.

"Take your time. She's fine here." The lady tells me where she is.

"I'll be there as soon as I can. Thanks for keeping her safe!" I hang up to the sound of a clap of thunder. I look out at the rain just as a bolt of lightning streaks through the sky.

Back home to grab the leash, I see the wind bang the side gate open and shut, open and shut. *So, that's how she got out!*

My drive to Shasta takes me eight blocks away to the other side of a big road. I pull into a strip mall in front of Nancy's Pet Parlor. A woman with a kind face steps out and greets me.

"You Shasta's mom? Come on in here out of the wet!" She flags me in.

"How'd you find her?"

She points down. "I heard her crying outside the door on the sidewalk. She was shivering and soaked." She smiles at me. "Good thing she had her fancy, heart-shaped nametag on. She's in the back, nice and dry now. What a sweet girl."

"Thank you for bringing her in and calling me. It's a miracle she got across that busy boulevard." I wave my hand at the cars as they race by.

"So that's where she came from? Yes, I see lots of accidents out there. That's no place for a dog, for sure. But she's a clever girl."

I sigh in relief. "The kids haven't even taken her for a walk down our street, so she wouldn't know her way home, either. God kept her safe. And you took her in. Thanks!"

"I couldn't let her stay out there, scared and wet. And she came right up to me as if I was a long lost friend. What a golden honeybun! Wait here, and I'll go get her."

The door opens, and she steps back in with Shasta, who looks like a new dog. She wears a paisley scarf, her step is light, and her fur is fluffed. When she nears me, I smell the scent of roses.

"Hope it's okay," Nancy begins. "I trimmed her nails and applied some cute Doggie Pawlish." It's true. Shasta's nails are bright pink to match her new neck gear, and she wags her tail.

"I gave this little lady our special doggie-day spa do-over." Nancy runs a hand over Shasta's back and then looks into my eyes from which a few tears have spilled and now roll down my cheek. "It's okay! It wasn't anything. My pleasure. On the house!"

My voice sticks in my throat, and I can't speak. I am struck by the way this kind woman has cared for our new girl. She not only brought her in from the storm but calmed her with the touch of love.

I clear my throat. "I thank you! And Shasta thanks you! And my kids thank you! You're an angel. A dog angel!"

Shasta and I trot through the rain to the car where she jumps onto the back seat.

I duck my head close to hers and rub her soft nose. "As for you, little lady, no visiting your new friend without permission. Your dog's day out is over!"

Damsel in Distress

by Susan Cheeves King

Early in my life, I began to see heroes come to my rescue when I was in a fix. The two who stick out most in my mind helped me when I was the most vulnerable — as a young woman in a far-off place. When I was nineteen and on my first flight out of the U.S., I met Dr. John Luh. Born in communist China, he was a professor of systems dynamics at Purdue University. His kindness began when he went with me on my train trip from the airport in Luxembourg all the way to my destination in Germany — just so he could help me get all my many bags off the train. Then, though he was on sabbatical in Stuttgart, he "fathered" me the entire four months that I was at Pepperdine University in Heidelberg. Once, he hosted a meal at a Yugoslavian restaurant in Stuttgart for fourteen of my school friends and me. Many times, he drove me and any friend of my choice to sights in Germany and Switzerland. Each time, he paid all the costs of our trip. Dr. Luh and I kept in touch until his death decades later.

My other hero story serves as a bookend to my stay in Europe, as it played out during my last days there. After my study in Heidelberg was over, I and some friends had spent a few weeks on trips to Italy and England. The day before I was to fly home found me alone in Paris at the Gare du Nord to buy the next day's train ticket to Luxembourg.

I had held back plenty of money to pay for my last days in Europe: the train fare, two meals for that day, then two more for the next — not to mention the cost of a place in Paris to spend the night. I also had to pay to "ransom" the luggage I'd placed in a locker in the Gare du Nord a week prior.

But my Eurail Pass had ended, and this was the only train fare I'd ever had to buy. I was crushed when the ticket turned out to cost much more than I had thought it would.

As I walked away from the ticket window, the light began to dawn on me that the money I had left could pay for a meal or two *or* to free my bags *or* maybe for a place to sleep — only one of these but not a thing more. I was in a fix.

This hard truth must have been all over my face when a voice to my side said in accented English, "May I help you?" Since I thought it might be a train official who would be open to giving me a discount, I began to detail my plight about not having the funds to pay for the rest of my trip home.

Then, mid-story, I raised my eyes to see a swarthy man who looked like a Turk. We school girls had been warned to avoid Turks since they seemed to go crazy when they got to a land where a woman could show her face or — gasp! — even her arms. All at once, the scary tales I had heard about Turkish sons sent to Europe to study began to flood my thoughts. In fact, in Dusseldorf, I myself had to swat away a swarm of young Turkish men — fresh off the Istanbul Express — when they began to pat and pet me.

So, with a catch in my voice, I cut my sad story short and then ended with, "Are you a Turk?" He told me that he was from Iran but lived in Paris. That and what he said next were music to my ears: "You don't need to worry. My name is Mahdi Armand,* and I will help you."

As usual for my naive self, I plunged in. "Really?" I said. "Do you speak French?" I told him that the main help I'd need would be for him to see if a room was free to rent at the cheap hotel where I'd stayed on my first trip to Paris. Thirty minutes in a phone booth later — and my purse many centimes lighter — our call still hadn't reached that hotel.

So, as I walked away, I told him I would just take the Metro there to see if any rooms were left. He then pulled out a Metro card and said he would pay our fare. At the front desk, we were told that all rooms were taken. Again, my hopes began to sink. On my other trip, I had gone to scores of hotels before I'd found one this cheap.

When he saw fear once again on my face, he said, "Don't worry. I live here in Paris. You can stay the night in my home." When I gave him a hard no, he said that his mother lived there as well. I still said no.

As we walked away from the hotel, he waved toward a cafe with an offer to buy me lunch. I jumped at that, as I thought, *That's one meal down.* After we left the cafe, my mind was in a frantic whirl of ideas, none of which would solve my plight. At the same time, I drowned in fear of the Iranian man who seemed stuck to me like a leech. All the way back to the Metro, I tried to get him to give up on his quest to "help" me, but to no avail.

Even I could see what he seemed to have in mind. At that thought, my eyes began to tear up. His own eyes showed deep stress as he asked me what was wrong. I began to list all my fears — going hungry, having to sleep in the train station, having to leave my bags there for good.

When he again began talk of my staying at his home, I turned to him as tears slid down my face. "But I am *innocent*," I said.

"You don't need to worry," he soothed. "I just want to help you. I work for the Iranian government." At that point, he pulled out his passport. "See," he said, pointing to the gilt lettering on its front, تامولپید. In his thick Persian accent, he read the French word under it: "Di-plo-mate." Then he set forth a plan. He would take me to a hotel, pay for it, and then leave.

"Would you really do that for me?" I asked, naive to the core.

We chose a hotel near the Gare du Nord so I would be safe when I went there early the next day. With its gold-trimmed columns, it was not a thing like my hotel on the Rue St. Jacques where I had to climb stairs to the next floor to get to the bathroom.

I felt my face go red when I gleaned the thoughts of the young man at the desk at the sight of this older Persian man paying for a room for a very young woman who had no bags with her. As we walked down the hall, his thoughts must have been confirmed when he saw that same man dog my heals as I went into the hotel room.

When I turned to see this man whom I had begun to trust as he stood there with his back up next to the door, my heart fell to my shoes. "I-I thought you said that you would find me a hotel room and then leave."

"Of course — later," he said.

All I could think of was to grab my purse to show him all my pictures of family back home. I hoped maybe this would remind him that he was a diplomat and I a young girl he was trying to help. While he looked at each photo and smiled, he made no move to leave.

"I don't think it's *proper* — Do you know the word, proper?" At the shake of his head, I said, "It's not right for you to be alone with me in my room."

He shrugged. "I will leave, but first I have a favor to ask."

At the word *favor*, my mind began to reel.

"I fly . . . tonight . . . London. Will you go . . . to . . . airport to say goodbye?"

"How will I get back?" I asked. Then he told me his plan. He would bring a friend with him when he came to the hotel to take me to the airport. There, he would buy me dinner (another meal checked off), and then the friend would take me to the train station, pay for my bags, then take me back to my hotel. After I thought about this, I said yes.

Hours later at my door, Mahdi introduced his very cute friend as Hamid Tajyk. As the friend sat mute near us on the bus trip to the airport, Mahdi and I talked about his life and my life.

A chink in the plans came when we found that the airport workers were on strike so no meals were to be had. Mahdi talked with Hamid in Farsi and then told me his new plan. Hamid would take me to dinner on the way to the train station. Then Hamid would leave once he saw me safe in the hotel lobby.

Just before he left to board the plane, Mahdi reached into a large bag he'd brought with him. "This is for your lunch tomorrow," he said, as he began to pull out item after item — a long French baguette, a drink, cheese, fruit, and a can of tuna. Then he put all the items back into the bag and gave it to me.

After I'd thanked him for all his help, he stood up and bowed. Then he took my hand, kissed it, and left to board the plane.

As soon as he was out of sight, Hamid came alive.

"I am so glad that tiresome man is gone!" he said, in perfect English. "Now I can have you all to myself."

We dined on the upper floor of a fancy restaurant with the lights of Paris spread out before us. Caught up in the mood, Hamid said, "I would love to buy you a swimming pool and fill it with champagne!" Failing that, he was going to make sure that I had a sumptuous multi-course meal to mark my last night in Paris.

It was also my last night in Europe — but not if Hamid had a say in it. He spent the rest of our meal trying to convince me to go with him to Vienna that night. He had an answer to my every demur:

"You could change your flight"

"You could cancel your ticket and just stay in Europe with me."

Later, as we stood at the front of the hotel, the glum Persian heaved a sigh and said, "Mahdi told me to take you to the hotel . . . and *leave*!" The look he cast my way still showed a slight ray of hope.

Shot down by the look I sent back, he reached for my hand, kissed it, and left. Back in my room, I thanked God for Mahdi and prayed for him to have a safe trip.

In the year that followed, Mahdi sent scores of letters and not a few gifts to my college mailbox. In time, he also shared his new plan with me: He would switch from Muslim to Christian, and then we would marry. He was crushed when I told him that I was pledged to marry someone else.

Even so, he asked me to send him all the material he would need to apply to a university near me in California where he could pursue his doctorate.

Before he was able to follow that plan, Iran's Shah fell from power at the hands of the Ayatollah Khomeini. At that time, all mail from Mahdi ceased, and my own notes were sent back marked, "No such address." Over the years that came next, I prayed for the life of this man who had been so loyal to the Shah — and so kind to me.

A year or two ago, on the Web, I found my dear Mahdi — alive and well and an Iranian envoy who served as president of an international council.

When I thought about my experience on those last days in Paris, an old adage kept going through my mind: "God takes care of fools and children."

I think I was a bit of both.

---

*Mahdi's real name has been changed because of rampant anti-American sentiment in the government of Iran.

25

Fast Friends

by Tina M. Hunt

My mother was ill from what we now think was COVID-19 but do not know for sure since this was before tests were widely used. I took care of her and when she got well, we had a talk. She was full of fear about the time when I would leave. Stress and angst filled her days and kept her from sleep. So my spouse, Nelson, and I had a long talk. We came to one mind, and now I live with and care for my mom while my spouse lives far off in our old home so that he can care for his mom.

To make me feel more at home here, Nelson brought a load of my things from home. But I ached to have my bike and could not bear the wait. So he shipped it to me. My joy knew no bounds! When I was sad and missed my husband, kids, and church; I would ride.

Then one day I had a flat tire. I did not know how to change or fix it. As I sat by the side of the road, I was so sad and felt so alone. I had one friend who lived too far away to help and no friends in my mother's town at all.

I saw lots of folks who rode bikes and thought one of them might help, but who to ask? At last I got up the nerve just to ask. A wife and her spouse were out for a ride and came by me when I was out for a walk. I had seen them many times so I waved them down and asked if they would or could help me. They were so kind and told me to come to their home.

So, I walked my bike the mile to their house. They met me at the door and at once made me feel at home. I was not known to them, yet their door was open wide and so were their hearts.

The spouse, Dave, made quick work to fix the tire, but also made sure I saw what he did step-by-step so I could fix it again if I had to. His voice was so calm, in spite of my lack of know-how, and my all-out bent to be a klutz. He did not laugh at me but helped me see that some humor makes the stress go and the work quick.

So now I have friends, Dave and Pat, in my new hometown. We wave and chat. I know if I have need they will be there. They taught me that good friends may be just folks we haven't met yet.

26

The Move to Be Kind

by Suzanne Nichols

Hot and tired, my husband and I took a break from our chores for a bite to eat at the local Wendy's. The chilled air made us want to stay, to put off going back into the July heat. So, long after the French fries were gone and our Frosty cups were empty, we sat in the cool place and watched the world go by.

As we sipped our sodas and wished we didn't have to leave, a young family came in and climbed into a booth near the door. Mom claimed one bench as Dad breezed off to place their food order. A boy of about eight years and a girl who looked to be about four shared the other bench.

Since their legs were too short to reach the floor, the children swung their flip-flop-clad feet back and forth below their tall perch. They leaned their heads on the back of the bench and fought the urge to close their eyes. The arms that hung limp at their sides were rosy and tanned, as were their cheeks and noses. Strands of dark blonde curls stuck out from their heads in wild waves — the mark of fun in the sun forced to end too soon.

Mom, too, looked tanned and rosy. I guessed they were all on their way home from a week at the beach.

Dad soon came with the meals and the family laughed and talked as they ate. I felt a bit like a spy, but it made me smile to see them enjoy this family time.

While they ate, a lean young man of about thirteen slid into the next booth. He sat with both feet on the bench and his back to the wall. His ears were plugged with ear buds and his head, crowned with tight, black curls, was bent over the phone he held with both hands.

I watched him for a long time. His only focus was the phone screen. But as soon as a woman with a baby girl stepped up to his booth, he laid down the phone and took out the ear buds. The woman held the baby in one arm as she slid onto the other bench. She spoke to the teen in soft tones as she searched in her tote bag with her free hand, then found some money and gave it to the young man who stood and walked away.

The woman reached into her bag again and found a bottle of milk. As soon as the baby girl caught sight of it, she squealed and pumped arms and legs the rich shade of cocoa. Two tiny teeth showed past her smooth mocha lips as she parted them to zone in on her milk.

Soon, the young man came to the booth with a tray of food. He put straws in the drinks and spread out the fries. They began to eat — he and the woman, who by now I had guessed was Mother to the two. With one hand she held her food; with the other, she held the bottle for the baby who lay in the crook of her arm.

The Beach Kids, of course, had to have Frostys to top off their meal. They hopped off the bench and went with Dad to place the order. Beach Mom turned from her seat toward the mother in the next booth.

"May I hold your baby while you eat? I can feed her for you."

Tired Mother looked up and smiled. And for the first time, I saw hope on a face that had, until then, seemed lined with care.

Teen Son slid over on the bench. Beach Mom took Baby Girl and sat down next to him. As Beach Mom fed Baby, Tired Mother ate. The two women shared small talk, and though I could not hear the words, I could see Tired Mother's face. The care seemed to fade, and her dark brown eyes soon glowed with fresh light.

All too often, I let life walk right past me and I just don't see it — people on their way to who-knows-where, doing what they want to do, or what they *have* to do. It's just too easy to not see them, to be busy with my own life, to focus on self and let the world go on by.

Beach Mom did not do that. She saw what I saw — but not with the same eyes. My focus was to relax, to eat in the cool, to delay going back into the heat. While I sat and only watched, she chose to act on what she saw. She took the step I did not take. She made the move to be kind.

A Good Kind of Strange

by Steve Duke

That day when I went to get my mail, I was stopped in my tracks. One item stood out since it had no stamp; and my wife's name, "Belinda," was written on it by hand. I called Belinda at work and told her about the strange piece of mail.

"Open it," she said.

"I don't open another person's mail," I told her.

"Go ahead and open it," she said.

I opened it to find a check — for $5,000 — from an older woman at church whom we didn't know very well and thought was poor. When Belinda got home from work, we agreed that she should call the woman and tell her we planned to give the check back.

"Miss Bessie," she began. "Steve and I received your check. Thank you, but we do not need it."

Miss Bessie's reply was short and to the point, "God told me to give it to you. Who are you or I to tell God that He is wrong?"

We couldn't argue with that. So Belinda and I came up with a new plan. The next day I went to the bank and got fifty one-hundred-dollar bills. Then at church, armed with the bills and a box of envelopes, I sought out those I felt could use a gift. With each, I would put a hundred-dollar bill into an envelope, hand it to a teen usher, and point to the one he should give it to. I told the teen to then walk away.

Over the next few nights moms, teens, and old folks got gifts. No one ever knew where the money had come from.

Bessie and I shared the same motto for life: When blessed, bless others.

Advice from a Stranger

by Sharon Fincannon

You'll never need an alarm clock again if you ask the Lord to awaken you each morning early enough to spend the time you need with Him," the stranger said. When this woman walked up to me, my husband and I were at a wake for the father of a man who'd worked for us.

I stared at her, in awe of the way she seemed to sense the pain in my heart. How could she know I lacked all hope that my life could change? After all, I'd never laid eyes on her before. Could she be why we were there?

She said she was the wife of the man who lost his dad and then told me her name.

For days, I'd cried out to the Lord for help, but no word had come. Then, at that wake, I felt that God had shown me the way through that stranger. He would have me go to Him to meet my needs.

As her words rang in my heart, I thought of Job and that God had allowed trials in his life but also reined in Satan's power. If that were true of Job, it could be true for me.

I also thought of Jesus and the times He rose before dawn to pray over His day.

Each day from that time on, I chose to seek God and spend time with Him. Again and again, He touched my heart and mind. He brought me peace, strength, joy, wisdom, and love.

God used that woman to help me face my trials with His strength. She changed my life and taught me that God does show His love for us — even through those we've just met.

By the Side of the Road

by Becky Hofstad

Our family, only days old, stood by the side of the main road through Lower Congo Town in Liberia, Africa. In the strong near-noon sun, we watched as taxi upon taxi passed. I bit my lip as a bead of sweat ran down my spine. Back home in the U.S., we had spent just shy of three years in pre-adoption "labor" and, at last, five year-old Naomi was ours. But, we still had four steep steps to climb in the next few days to board a plane to take her with us to Minnesota.

This was Monday. We had to get the doctor to sign off on Naomi's health exam. I'd heard her wail for the first time last week when the nurse pricked her finger for a blood draw, so the exam was done; but we were still short the signed form to prove it. Without the form, her visa could not be made final. Once we had her visa, we still weren't done. Two agents of the Liberian government — each in his or her own post — would have to sign off to make way for Naomi to go home with us. Our first stop was to see the doctor, who was due back in town mid-day. In the midst of car honks that blared at all times of the night and day in this city, I pled with God, "Please don't let this doctor be late."

At the start of our day, my husband had sat at the round table in our leased flat. Our new daughter was on his lap, both of them still in their clothes for sleep. Mike had turned the LCD pane on the camera so that he could film Naomi while at the same time she could see her own image in the small screen. She moved her lips in and out as if for a kiss, raised her thin brows above her eyes, and squealed with joy to see her own moves in real time.

I watched the scene as I peeled boiled eggs to take with us to town for a snack. Naomi's bond with her new dad brought to mind that God's plans are more grand than any I can make.

My thoughts were put on hold by a phone call from the man we'd hired to drive us here and there. He said he was on the wrong side of a protest and wouldn't make it to us in time. Last week when he was ill, we'd found a taxi. I felt strain in my neck as I thought about that ride. When at last a car did stop, we were told there was room for only one. Mike stayed firm that all three of us had to stay in one group. And soon, the three of us were packed in with three other adults and two small kids in a tight ride share. It is the norm, we soon found out, that Americans are not asked to share. They know that we like our space.

Now, as we stood near the front gate of our flat with the young guard in a white shirt, we were tense. We had to get to the clinic. As each taxi passed the three of us, we didn't blame the guard for our bad luck. No taxi wants to miss out on fares, to go less than full.

Mike held Naomi so she could see, her thin legs bent at the knee over his arm. As I took in the image, I felt a pang in my chest from worry that we wouldn't make it. When we said we'd adopt Naomi, we knew she had not put one foot in front of the other, on her own, ever. What we didn't know was the cause. Nor did we know what other health issue she might have. We were urged on by our strong drive to get Naomi on a plane to the States where in next-to-no time, she could have an MRI (not an option in Liberia).

All at once, the guard left us and ran toward a blue four-door car, fifty feet up on the same side of the street. In a short time, he had news for us, "Those men will take you."

Did I dare let the wave of calm swell in my chest as the car came near? Two Liberian men were in the front seat, neatly dressed in slacks and polo shirts. They smiled. Through the now-open back door, Mike said hi.

"You're able to take us to Monrovia, to the clinic?" he said. A shared glance showed that Mike and I had no choice but to take this ride. The three of us got into the back seat of the car that had seemed to show up out of thin air. Would we be safe? Where would we end up? We didn't know. But, we knew that our daughter couldn't wait.

Mike and I talked with the men as Naomi put her hands in my hair, then on my cheeks. Mike shared our adoption story while I took time to think on why men we didn't know would do this for us. *Do they sense our need or just wish to spread warm cheer?* I thought. *Or did God send them from above?*

The two who were our help made it through the stop-and-go traffic with ease. As the car came up the street near the clinic, the men would not take any cash. To us, a "thank you" was not enough, and yet it was all we had. Why did they do it? We would never find out.

30

More Than a Drink

by Lauren Craft

rash.

The jolt came as fast as the light changed.

My friend had begun to turn left on green but did not yield to the cars going straight. Now his car had merged with the other car to trash the road ahead with metal.

My blood raced. My hands shook. I was a teen and had never been in a wreck before.

We stepped out in the hot night air. A lady and three kids were in the van that my friend hit. All were okay — not one cut or bruise — but my pulse still thumped.

Red and blue lights came. The July air was damp, even at that late hour. Time dragged on and on.

Soon my nerves calmed, but I ached.

When can we go home? I wiped sweat from my brow. I longed for my bed. My throat as dry as sand, I craved a cold drink.

Soon, a man about my dad's age stopped at the scene. "You all okay?" he asked. We said yes and thanked him.

He walked back, reached for his car door, then paused.

"You know," he called to us. "I have a cooler full of sodas in the trunk. Anyone want one?"

My eyes grew wide. "I'd love one!"

After my thanks, he smiled and drove away. I took a sip from the cold can.

Soon, the cars were towed. Forms were penned and signed. Glass was cleaned off the street.

My thirst had been quenched by that long-gone drink.

The scene was almost back to usual.

But one thing stayed in my mind: that man's kind heart.

It may seem a small thing; but to me at that point on that night his offer was huge.

When he saw our car, the man could have thought, *They have lots of help. Just head home.* Or later, *Don't ask them about a drink at a time like this.* But he didn't.

His heart led him to take the time to pull over. His heart spawned an idea and then didn't reject it even though it seemed so small. The man with that heart knew just one way to help — and cared enough to ask.

31

When in Rome . . .

by Alyssa Wedemeyer

Just a few days back, I didn't even know this girl. Now she held my hair from my face as I puked down the aisle of a full bus tour in Europe. The year was 2018 and I was in Italy on a class trip to learn of Paul of Tarsus and what he did while in Rome. Her name was Kelsey, and she was a saint from the south. She began as a stranger and that day turned into a dear friend. That's when she showed me the heart of Christ. Since then, I have yearned to give that kind of love every day of my life. At the time, I knew no more of her than her name and the town she was from.

It was on the last day of our Rome tour and Kelsey shared a seat with me. All at once, my gut felt weird and my head bowed down as though the weight of an anvil. Right then, I knew that I would be sick.

Not here! I thought. Please, God, anywhere but here. I haven't been sick in so long. I don't want to puke all over this bus in front of forty people I don't know! At least let me get back to my room to do this in private!

And then . . .

I stretched across poor Kelsey's lap — since she had the seat on the end — and hurled into the aisle. Seven times.

She didn't so much as pause but rushed to pull my hair back from my face. She rubbed my back and helped take off my coat as it had taken a hit from the spray. After I left the bus to go up to my room to rest, she stayed late to clean up the mess I'd made in the aisle.

I was shocked. How could a person I did not know make it a point to care for me like that? I chewed over it for days. I felt humbled when the answer came to me: love. Christ's love. Kelsey had allowed Christ's deep love to shine through her to me. The same love He has for all God's children — His brothers and sisters. That day His grace became real to me.

The kindness of a stranger can change your life. I know it did mine.

32

To Restore a Son

by Dan Lewis

M any times, I have seen the way God shows His love for us through the people in our lives. When I was in my senior year of high school, one of my teachers paid for me to take a trip to visit the University of Miami in Florida when she heard that I couldn't afford it.

Her all-expense-paid gift changed the course of my life.

My senior year of college, I read a book by Elisabeth Elliot.* This author's life story nudged me to go on a mission trip. The rules did not allow me to go without a team, so a couple from church went with me to spend four weeks teaching English in Argentina using the Bible. There, those two helped me learn to love being an active part of God's church. Our paths crossed for only a brief span of my life, but God used this trip to build in me a passion for ministry.

Every day since February 21, 2020, I see God in the acts of kindness and love of not only long-time friends but also total strangers.

On that day, while riding on his skateboard with school friends from Biola University, our oldest son, Nate (age 18) was hit by a truck. In the months since that head injury, he has been in a minimally conscious state. In spite of surgeries and other medical procedures, we're still not sure if our dearly loved son even knows we're there.

Yet, through all of it, God has kept our faith strong every day as we care for him. "We" are his mother and I and our son, Matt, and Nate's girlfriend, Camille.

But with us stand an army who prays with us and does so much more. Many of them started out as strangers.

One Sunday, at a church in Oceanside, that we have never been to, the pastor, whom we have never met, stopped in the middle of his sermon to pray for Nate, whom he didn't know.

Shortly after Nate's accident, when we put out the call for help with funds, we were awed by the level and source of what was given. One family we've never met pledged to give every month — which they still do — even though the husband was out of work. Another family who live across the country sent us their stimulus check.

About one-fourth of the meals made for us through our church's "Meal Train" were from people we had never met prior to Nate's accident.

Since that Friday night in February, people we don't know have donated medical equipment, sent words of cheer, mailed Nate birthday cards, spurred us on in our faith when we began to fall under the load, and prayed for us every day.

At times, I just don't get it. I don't get why Nate's story has become a thing. I don't get why our little-boy-turned-young man who was hurt in such a dire way has rallied so many troops, prayer warriors, and spiritual powerhouses to add their food, finances, and faith to ours when ours seemed so insufficient. I don't know why people numbering in the hundreds keep reading my journals in Caring Bridge and keep praying and checking in on us. Just the thought that so many people — many of whom I may never meet in person — pray and love on our son brings tears to my eyes. I am stunned, I am honored, I am in awe.

And, because of these hundreds of people I didn't know prior to February 21st, our extended Lewis family has grown in numbers and in love!

Over these many months, two "strangers-turned-friends" have linked their lives with ours in a special way.

One such kind stranger is Jenn who touched us with the prayers she would post online. Then one night she showed up at University of California, Irvine Medical Center with a huge gift basket for us that came with very special gifts for each of us. It also had one to give away which we did to a family whose son was in the Neuro ICU wing at UCI at the same time as ours.

Jenn is a Prayer Warrior like none I have known before. Her Spirit-filled prayers stir us and come straight out of the Word of God. I like to say she "prayer stalks" us as often she would come to the hospital and now the doctor's office to pray outside during our appointments. She has brought people together online and in person to pray for Nate every day.

We all know that it isn't Jenn but God doing the work through her. But Jenn's prayers, words of encouragement, and scripture have served to carry us through many of our crises times over these many months. She has helped to move spiritual mountains that we couldn't seem to scale or move on our own.

And, the crazy thing is, we didn't know her prior to Nate's accident! Yet, the love and kindness of this stranger-turned-friend has touched our lives more than we can ever voice or even know.

Kristen is the other stranger-turned-friend member of our close-in Prayer Warrior Team.

The first time Kristen came into our view was when she brought us a meal and asked if she could sit in her car outside our house and pray for us. Then she did it again . . . and again . . . and again! It was clear to us that this woman was about praying for us and soon she had made her way into our prayer family. She still brings us our meal every Tuesday night and prays over Nate while we eat. She likes to use us as "guinea pigs" for her meals and, once — over a span of many weeks — took us on a culinary trip around the world that was hands down tasty.

When Kristen prays in our home, she lays her hands lovingly on Nate — at times his head, at times his arm — and prays in hushed tones. Seeing the bond she has with the Spirit lifts us up.

Many more such strangers-turned-friends lift us up, spur us on, pray for us, and serve as the wind under our wings. Though they began as strangers, they still knew us because God knows us; they cared about us because God cares about us; they are part of Nate's story because Nate's story is part of the same God Story that we all share.

Romans 12:9-13 sums up the people who have come into our lives these past months. In the NRSV, this section is titled, "The Mark of the True Christian." Our friends — both new and old — have shown these marks of the true Christian to the max. We pray that one day we can meet those new friends. Be it this side of heaven or when we are with the King — along with Nate restored here or there — we bask in their love and kindness. It has changed our lives forever.

How God must smile as He sees His people uniting on our knees to Him!

#RestoreNate

Passion and Purity: Learning to Bring Your Love Life under Christ's Control

33

Vote Today 2020

by Ann L. Coker

I saw the date in a book — Tuesday, June 2 — and had to look up why it rang a bell. Primary day in Indiana: the day to vote for who would run in the November 2020 election. Online, I found the place where we were to vote: a church close by. I told my husband, Bill, to get his ID, for he would need it at the polls.

When we got to the church, we saw many cars parked in the lot which was also ringed by a very long line of voters. As we walked to find the end of the line, Bill asked, "Why?" over and over again. With his Alzheimer's, he could not make sense of what we were doing. To vote began to seem less and less of a good plan for that day, so I told him that we would go home. As we turned to head to the car, a couple near us said, "Take our place, and we will go to the end of the line."

I was not sure, but they urged me again with, "No, take our place." We didn't know them, but we got in line, about twenty feet from the door. Then a new couple ahead of us said, "Here, get in front of us," I thanked them. With my mind tuned to Bill and his needs, I did not say more to any of our new friends. I regret that.

This was June, 2020, so COVID-19 made "social distancing" the order of the day. Lines on the ground both outside and in kept us six feet apart. Most wore masks. A young man at the church door let in a few at a time. In reply to Bill's query, I tried to help him see why we had to keep back. "Look at the others. Nobody is standing close to strangers."

As we stood in front of the poll worker, I asked if Bill could be with me at the booth and told why. He said yes, and I thanked him. We voted, and on the way out a worker thanked us. We stopped at McDonald's for carry-out, one of Bill's best treats.

Back home, my mind was at peace as I thought about the day's long list of those who had reached out to be kind to a woman torn between the value she placed on the right to vote and on the husband who needs her more than ever.

Though we did not know each other, all those who helped us did know that we share a common bond of love for our "land of the free and home of the brave."

34

Tools Plus Heart

by Jennifer Aaron

My day was not going well. First, I had to shop with my twin toddlers, which was never easy. Then, I got to the checkout, and my credit card was turned down. I didn't have cash to cover my items, and this small store had no ATM. Back went my items to their shelves. Angry and embarrassed, I swept my girls out to our van. I plopped my purse down on the floor while I strapped the girls into their car seats, then slammed the door closed. A split second too late, I saw that I had locked their door, as I always did, but that I hadn't picked up my purse first, as I always do. My day had just gone from bad to worse.

Cell phones were still rare, so I didn't have one stuck in my jeans. My only choice was to go back into the store I had just left and admit to a jam worse than a credit card being turned down. I called my husband, who was over half an hour away. The clerk said a fire truck might have the tool to open my door, so I called them too. I didn't call a locksmith since we didn't have a penny to spare. The day was cool and cloudy, so the girls wouldn't be harmed by the time in the car. I went back to my van to wait for my husband and watch over my poor girls. Though I was a wreck, they were calm. Two fire trucks came, plus a police car, but none of them could help me. As the firemen were about to leave, my hero came.

The white steed he rode in on was a locksmith's truck. He got out and took no time at all to pop open my car door. He told me he had seen the swarm of emergency trucks and guessed why they had grouped in the lot. Then he chose to come out of his way get the car open for us. Though this was his work, he wouldn't let me pay him. He said he got a few calls each year for kids trapped in cars and never charged for those jobs. I was so upset with myself, but he was calm and nice. If he had been harsh with me, my heart would have stayed heavy even after my babies were free. But he let me know that I wasn't the first mom to lock herself out and her kids in. With what he did and what he said, he turned my day around. True, it was an act that anyone with the right tool could have done, and he spent only a few minutes with us. But the way he helped us is so set in my mind that I still think of his kind act — even twenty-eight years later.

35

God's Eye on Us

by Briana Novacek

Dad and I were on our way to Milwaukee's Froedtert Hospital to see Mom. After four weeks in a coma due to a rare issue from Influenza A, my mom had been moved to a new room.

The past few months had been so hard, but when Mom woke from her coma on Easter morn, we felt hope in the light to come.

Now, on that bright, sunny day as my dad and I drove to bring her home, we jammed to the radio. But when our drive was only half over, the car broke down. This was pre-cell phones, of course. And the house or two that we could see were too far away to reach. Still, we began to walk along the road, going north. I wasn't sure what the plan was, but Dad knew, so I wasn't scared. I was only eight years old, so if Dad was in charge I felt calm. He must have been scared, though, his mind busy with thoughts of how we would get home.

Not much later, a car pulled over, and a woman yelled out, "Do you need a ride?" The back seat of her small sedan was packed full, so Dad and I both squeezed into the front, and I sat on his lap. On our drive, the kind lady asked us where we were going and about our lives. She drove us about half an hour all the way back to our house. That ride alone made us feel cared for. It showed us that God had His eye on us.

But the woman didn't stop with just the drive home. She got in touch with her church friends and let them know about us. Soon after, food began to come in our front door from more people we did not know. The fridge was full to the seams with food. Dad said it was just about too much for us to eat, even though by that time Mom was home. She says some of the food seemed to just show up in our fridge.

Dad said he was not used to this kind of act. Often we put our guard up and try to take care of our own family. But it can be so good to trust those who want to help, to let go of your own pride and let them serve you.

Dad and I were just over the moon that Mom was home so our family was in one piece again. Mom was not the same as the old Mom, but she would be in time. Her hair was thin and didn't lie the way it used to. She got tired often and had to rest. So I would grab my small stool and perch it right next to her spot on the couch and talk to her. I didn't need her to do any one thing but just be. I just wanted to be near her, to breathe the same air, to share the same space. To have Mom at home after so much time with her in a cold, white room away from us felt like pure joy to me. God had brought her back to us.

Now, over twenty years later, I look back on that year when Mom was sick as one of the most vital times of my life. It shaped who I would later be. It gave my mom and me a strong, deep bond that has never left me.

In that time of trial, many kind folks cared for our family. The kind woman who gave us a ride home and brought us meals was such a sweet soul. But she brought with her many more. Our lives were filled with those who cared so fully for us and yet did not know us fully. All of those who cared for us — at the hospital and at home — made us feel that we were not alone. As they lived out their faith in love, we felt the touch of God.

I want to be the kind of person who cares. For people I don't know, for the lost, for the close and the far.

36

What Color Are Angels?

by Reba Rhyne

Now if you think I have an inner track on the reply to this query, you would be right. I do. Not all angels are white with white wings. Some are black and they drive small Chevy trucks.

Many years back as an expert working in the boating trade, I would go to shows and man, or "woman," a booth selling my skills in making and building boat upholstery. I'd pack my car's trunk with the items needed for my booth and head out — some of the time to Orlando, or Miami, or Atlanta.

As a single woman on the road much of the time, I knew I had to avoid any break downs on my trip. So I drove a newer car with low miles. Also, in the back seat, I would pack snacks and the needs for staying in town or with friends. In other words, this four-tired piece of metal was always packed full.

This one show was at the Georgia World Congress Center in Atlanta, next to the Omni Hotel. No, I wasn't staying there, as it's too rich for my blood. After finding my booth and unloading much of my show items, I got back on the road and headed on south for Macon, Georgia on Interstate 75, where I would stay at a friend's house. I planned to drive back and forth each day.

Traffic was heavy, but in the Atlanta area you have to drive the speed that all cars are going or you get run over.

A semi-truck was far ahead of me and a motorcycle right in front. Suddenly, the truck flipped a black object in the road, which the rider on the bike swerved to barely miss. It turned out to be a long slice of injection-molded plastic which is ridged and deadly on tires, especially this one — the type that had jagged points. I had no way to avoid the chunk that flew under my car. As I ran over the part, my left-rear tire went flat.

From the middle of the three-lane road, I started easing my car to the right lane. Then I was able to pull over and park in the shade under a bridge that stretched over the interstate. I saw that two more cars with flat tires had pulled over but in the hot sun.

There was nothing to do but for all of us to wait for help. I got out of the car and stood off on the shoulder. I didn't have a cell phone or a way to contact anyone for help. Finally, a Georgia State Trooper appeared and stopped at the other cars. When he pulled back into the flow of cars, he went right by me. Amazed, I looked at his tail lights and thought, *Why did he pass me by?*

Soon I would find out. It was God's plan to pave the way for my black angel to show up. He slowed and it took some feet for him to come to a stop in the fast-moving traffic. He backed up, got out of his truck, and offered me his cell phone.

"I don't know a single person in Atlanta," I told him and shook my head.

"Hmmmm," he said. "Where is your spare tire?"

Did he really want to know? We moved items out of the trunk and found the tire. The trunk held no jack, but he had one.

As the Atlanta traffic whipped by, he changed the flat tire for that small kind you use until you can buy a new one. But my small tire was mostly flat.

"You mustn't drive on this tire," he said. "Three exits down, there's a gas station where we can fill it with air. Just follow me."

"Okay." Even though I didn't know this man from Adam, I felt as if I could trust him.

As he filled the tire with air, I asked him where he worked. He was an instructor at the diesel school in the city. When I offered him some money, he turned it down.

"It wouldn't look good for a white lady and a black man to be fighting over money in a parking lot," I said, with the hope that he would change his mind.

He still refused the money, but added, "If my mother has a problem out on the road in her car, I hope someone will be nice and stop to help her."

In place of a fight, I gave him a heartfelt hug. He got in his truck and left.

Do I know about angels? Yes, I surely do. Was he human or an angel? You judge. After all, the Bible does say that at times we may not know when we are with an angel: *Do not forget to show hospitality to strangers, for by so doing some people have shown hospitality to angels without knowing it* (Hebrews 13:2 NIV).

Twenty-five years, I still think of this kind young man; and each time, I say a little prayer for him . . . and his mother.

37

The Sign-Off

by Ann Clark Van Hine

OCTOBER, 2001

Cards, cards, and more cards. Some from those I knew, others from those I'd never met. Many missing my house number or zip code. Each held words that bid me peace, hope, or help in a time of grief. Each were dear to me, but one ended in a way that made me gasp — "from a concerned Gramma in Oklahoma — Nita" My father's mother once lived in Oklahoma. She was long gone; but this felt like a hug, a nod, a wink from the ages, a link to the past. The words of the note were a gift as well: *The tragedy of last month has touched me deeply, as it has most of America. I wanted so to be helpful in some way for those who were directly effected. I called the Nazarene headquarters in Kansas City, (I am a member of the Nazarene Church) and asked for the phone number of the Nazarene district office in New York where the tragedy happened. . . . And Ann since then I've asked God to be with you and comfort you. I am so very sorry. . . ."*

I wrote and told Nita how much her sign off had meant to me since it made me think of my much-loved grandmother from Oklahoma. Nita's reply told of her sense that she was to sign the card as she had. She didn't see the value in it at the time but still did it. Now she knew why.

At Christmas, Nita sent a box of items she had made with her own hands. A small tree, a star or two or ten out of white paper, old Christmas cards made into tiny boxes — each sent to my family as a token of love. For many years, Nita and I wrote back and forth. Then, when a note came from her daughter that told of Nita's death, I shed tears for her and her family.

Now each Christmas as I place her small tree in its place of honor, I go back in my mind to her first note, to her sign off, to her love for her God and her kind act to me. Thank you, "Grandma" Nita.

38

Saving the Day — and My Summer

by Adam Benson

One summer while I was in college, I took a job in Yosemite National Park as a lobby porter at the Lodge at the Falls, which means I helped folks with their bags and I cleaned. And one of my jobs that summer was to clean the pool restrooms. My boss, Doug, had a *right* way he wanted me to clean them, but let's just say . . . I took some short cuts. I don't want to get into all the "why's" or "why not's," but I was in my 20's, I was a male, and I liked to talk to the girls by the pool. That says it all.

On this day, one of the guests went to speak to the manager of the hotel (Doug's boss) about how gross and dirty the pool restrooms were. I was shocked to hear my name on the walkie-talkie: "Doug and Adam, please report to Karl's office now." I knew this was bad, because we did not get calls to go talk with the Big Boss — ever. So, there we were, in chairs in front of Karl's huge desk with The Man on the other side. At that time, I feared for my life, my job, my name, and my summer. At first, Karl did not say one thing but just looked at Doug in a way that said, "What are we going to do with him? Should we fire him?" Doug just sat there with a calm look on his face while I looked at him, scared out of my mind.

At this point in the summer, Doug and I did not know each other that well. So here I was about to lose my job and my summer. I would have to go home, and I *loved* Yosemite — so much. I did not want to be sent back home, but I was sure I was about to. My mother and father would be angry *at* me and also sad *for* me. Karl went on a mad rant for a while, then asked Doug, "What should we do with him?" Three or four seconds felt like a long time, as Karl sat there and waited.

And then Doug said, "It's my fault. I take the blame for this one. There were a few things I did not teach him, and that is on me, but it will not happen, again." That, of course, was not true. Doug had lied for me so I could keep my job and save face. At this point, Karl was shocked, and so was I — in part because Doug never messed up. We all knew this: Doug was good at his job and never messed up. And he didn't mess up this time; I did! But, he took the blame for me, and I was off the hook. So Karl let me stay. Doug took on the shame and the blame of what I had done, so that I could keep my job and good name and stay in Yosemite, a place of so much life and joy. What Doug did was pure grace, Jesus-like grace.

At one point I had sensed that my boss loved Jesus, and I was proved right on this later — as over the months we became friends. And, this was one of those times when someone was Jesus to me, a person whom I barely knew up until this point. In a very real way, Doug helped me to taste and see that the Lord is good.

39

Made with Love
and Prayers

by Karen Woodard

A box came in the mail for my four-year-old son, Ben. It was a large, heavy box from a lady whose name I did not know. I thought at first that the box had come to my son in error. We had not placed a mail order and had not been in wait for a large piece of mail. But again, I read my son's first and last name, our post box, town, state, and zip code.

Ben couldn't wait to get the box home and rip into it. We sat it on the table, and when the box was freed from the tape, Ben pulled it open to a sea of green, which he thinks is the best color in the world. He pulled the green mound from the box and saw that it was an afghan about the size of a twin bed. The ends were fringed, and it was made in single crochet, a stitch that takes a great deal of time and care. With the afghan was a note that read in part, "Made with love and prayers from Brenda."

A few months prior, Ben had suffered a TBI (traumatic brain injury) and was in the hospital for a month. I found out later that Brenda had begun to pray for Ben at that time and prayed for him each day as she stitched the afghan. She had even taken an extra step to find out what color Ben liked best. When the last stitch was done, she took the afghan to the altar of her church and asked the saints that were there that day to join her at the altar to pray.

From that time on, each night when I tucked Ben in under the cover of all the love and prayers that came with the afghan, my heart was at peace. Her gift blessed our family a great deal. Brenda's kind acts moved me to use my gifts to bless others. I too began to pray for folks, even when they're not aware, and even if we don't know each other — just as this ex-stranger did for Ben and our family.

Prayer was truly a gift that helped my family through dark days. Every day God moves through hearts to bring help to us in that way. When we are at the end of our strength and hopes have faded, He uses His saints to draw us back to Him and His love. My goal now is to act when God shows me a need. If it be prayer, a gift one can touch, or both that I choose to bless a soul with; I have no doubt that each kind act — great or small — begins with a nudge from God. And my faith tells me that when God gives a nudge and I act on what He leads me to do, He never fails to make it grow ten-fold.

I hope we can all aim to spread God's light in a world that's grown dark for many. If we work to that end, our kind acts will form a chain of hope, like that afghan stitched with prayer.

Hebrews 6:19 NIV: *We have this hope [set before us] as an anchor for the soul, firm and secure.*

Yule Love

by Karen Dorsey

Oh no! My mind spun. I had the wrong card. A huge pile of Christmas food and goods lay on the belt in front of me. This store took only cash or bank cards. The line in back of me grew long as I spoke to the clerk.

"No problem," said the clerk. "Just bag up your groceries, and I'll take them to customer service. You can come back and pay for them later."

With a red face, I put the food in bags and thought of the long drive home and back. I would come to this store only when I was going to be near it for other things. I had chores at home to do.

Then I heard a sound behind me. "Merry Christmas," said the clerk with a smile. She gave me my sales slip. "The man behind you in line just paid your bill."

Shock ran through me. *He what?*

"It's Christmas . . . and I had some extra money," the man said. "I wanted to share with someone."

"I'm speechless. Th-thank you." I thought of all the extra treats I'd bought. This bill was huge.

"I really did want to do something for someone this year," he said again. "You just gave me the chance."

"I don't know what to say. You are so kind. And so thoughtful. You have blessed me."

"It's okay. I feel blessed to be able to do this."

I left the store, still with a red face but also with light steps and a heart full of warmth and joy. A man that I did not know had shown me the love that Christmas is all about.

Color Blind

by Patti Conn

It was 2020. The great shift that took place that year began with the COVID-19 pandemic. Then came march after march for equal rights for blacks, which soon turned to riots. Every day the media told of the havoc and the chaos blow by blow, and many — both white and black — were on edge. It wasn't hard for me — or any of us — to lose focus.

After the pandemic began, just a trip to the store — which I had come to enjoy since my recent retirement — had turned into a chore. We had to wear masks, use hand sanitizer, stay six feet apart at all times — all to find that many of the basic items we might need were not there to buy. Then once home, we had to wash some things.

On my trip of the week to the store. I was all set with mask, sanitizer, and umbrella for the storm to come. All went well, but at the store's exit I saw that a doozy of a storm had hit. The rain fell in heavy sheets. With two zips to my purse, I made sure the things in it would stay dry. Umbrella open and keys in hand, I dashed to my car, where I threw my soaked bags in the trunk as fast as I could. By the time I was done, I was as wet and cold as my bags. I shut the trunk and returned my cart. Then I flew back to my car, threw in my umbrella as I climbed in, then shut the door in haste. I had to free up the space for a car behind me.

As I drove home, my mind and eyes were trained on the road as the heavy rain made it hard to see. Back at our house, I looked down at the seat next to me and saw — nothing. No purse. My heart sank. In all that wet mess I'd had to deal with, I must have left my purse in the cart.

I raced back to the store, a prayer on my lips all the way. The staff was kind, but no one had seen my purse. And now, after going into the store and back out again in the rain, I was not only glum and soaked but chilled to boot. I prayed again as I drove back home, but all I could think of was what I would need to do if my purse was gone for good. Not the least of my woes was that I had lost my brand-new cell phone.

When I walked through the door of our home, what I saw blew me away. There, right in front of me on our kitchen counter, sat my purse! I was in shock, I asked my husband, "How on earth did my purse get here?"

With a big smile, he told me that a tall, young black man had come to the door and said that he had seen my purse in a cart out in the rain. He found my ID and where we live and drove two miles in the storm to our house to bring it to me. At first, my husband had been a bit dazed, as he didn't even know I'd lost my purse. But he thanked the young man and they shook hands — in spite of the Covid rule to keep six feet apart. As the young man walked away, my husband thanked God, too.

I was thrilled! While I searched to find my purse, God had been at work. I was full of fresh hope, too. Even in this rough patch for the black and white races, a young black man had come to the aid of an older white woman. He chose to take the high road. What a model for us all!

The Car Angel

by Janet Asbridge

The day our seventeen-year-old son, Danny, paid off his first car, I baked him a pumpkin pie to let him know how proud I was of him. He'd worked hard to earn the cash for that old Honda Accord.

One week later, he called to tell us that he was stuck at the Indoor Skate Park. The car wouldn't start. My husband, Bob, and I were upset. Good things always seemed just out of Danny's reach. Here was more of the same. It didn't seem fair.

I prayed as we drove to the skate park. *Danny has worked so hard for that car. Why can't things ever go his way? Please help.*

At the park, Danny stood near the car with a scowl on his face. His dad tried but couldn't get it started. He called a tow truck.

Bob told him he would try to fix it but that Danny had to watch and learn. The whole way home, Danny didn't say a word.

The next morning, Bob woke him up early, "Let's get to work."

Danny's face was glum as he watched Bob work under the hood. A while later, they went to the parts store and came home to work on it some more.

I cheered when the car roared to life. They took off for a test drive around the block. A short time later, I saw them pushing the car back down our long driveway. Danny's face looked like a dark cloud as he stormed to his room.

Bob called auto shops to ask them about it. They told him that the car could not be fixed.

My heart ached for Danny, and I prayed that God would send

help. But all seemed lost that night after dinner as Bob taught him a new task: how to write an ad and post it on Craig's List: "Honda Accord for parts. $600 or best offer."

A few days later, a man called about the car. Bob was out of town for work, so Danny asked him to call back the next night.

"At least you'll have $600," I said when he hung up. "After a while, you'll have enough to buy a new one."

Danny just shrugged. "I worked hard for that car, Mom."

The next day, as I got ready for work, I was rushed and stressed. I had to drop Danny off at school before I went to my job. I was late. The phone rang on my way to the shower.

"Hello?"

"I talked to your son last night about the Honda Accord you have for sale," came the slow-talking voice. "I would like to come look at it now."

"My husband isn't home, and he's the one you need to talk to about it. Can you come look at it tonight?"

"I would like to look at it now." The man's voice seemed to slow down even more.

"We have to leave the house in half an hour," I said in a rush. "No one will be here to show it to you."

"I would like to look at it now," the man said again.

I didn't want to kill a sale. Danny needed the money. Who knew if anyone else would want it? Plus, I had to get off the phone so I could dress for work. "Okay. Come on over."

As I backed the car out of the garage, Danny and I saw an elderly man looking under the hood of the Honda. He waved and his kind eyes glowed. We waved back, glad that he looked like a nice guy.

That night the phone rang, and Bob picked it up. I heard him say, "Uh huh. Is that right? Okay thank you. I will try it."

When he hung up, he said, "It was the guy who looked at

the car. He told me how to fix it. He says only one brand of part works to fix that model of Honda Accord."

I laughed. "Do you think he knows more than a mechanic does?"

"What he said makes sense. It's worth a try," said Bob.

After a trip to the car-parts store and a bit more work, Bob and Danny drove off in the car for a test drive. This time, it rode fine.

When they came into the house, we laughed.

I asked, "What do you think? Did God send an angel to show you how to fix your car, just so you'd know He loves you?"

I hadn't seen Danny's face that bright in more than a year. He smiled. "Yeah," he said. "Maybe he did."

43

Left Behind

by Liz Kimmel

L ife as the sixth child out of seven had its ups and downs. At times the older kids would want to play with me; at times no one would pay me any mind. This is the tale of one of those days.

Even though he wasn't pastoring our church at the time, every Sunday my dad chose to be one of the first to come and the last to leave. As the day began, our parents would round up all seven of us and herd us into the old woody wagon. That was no easy feat. The three big boys would drag their feet, and the girls would delay us with their need for more time to dress up and fix their hair. My oldest sister helped Mom get all three of us girls ready to go. And of course the baby would take his own sweet time to eat and burp and mess his pants and make Mom change his clothes a bunch of times.

Once we'd all piled in (no seat belts — just packed like fish in a can), Dad would start the car and pull away from the curb. Church was only five miles away. But prior to that short trip, we had to go north a ways and pick up two or three men from Bethel Seminary, which upped our total to twelve of us squished into a space meant for nine.

When we got to church, we would try to un-stick our limbs from each other and would then swarm out of our car like clowns in a circus. For those who watched, it was quite a sight as more and more of us would roll out onto the street. And then we each went our own way — Dad to do his usher duty, Mom to take care of the baby, and the rest of us kids to who-knows-where, to do who-knows-what. I missed some of the fine points of the story, since I was only four at the time.

On this day, church and Sunday school were over, but no one came to pick me up so I played alone for much more time than usual. When the teacher's head was turned away, I snuck out the door and went in search of my clan. They weren't in the large room where the altar was. Mom wasn't in the nursery. The big kids weren't in the rooms where they met for their class. As I came into the lobby, I glanced out the front doors to see our big old car as it pulled away from the curb.

I ran toward them, called after them, waved my arms in alarm. But they didn't see me. I stood on the walk in shock as the tears began to flow. What else was a four year old to do? Lucky for me, a kind man came along and knelt down to pick me up. I have no idea who he was. The church doors weren't open any more. My dad had locked them as they left for home. But this stranger was a smart man. Even though no one had cell phones when this event took place, this man found a phone and called the police.

Until they came, he calmed my fears and soothed my nerves. My tears dried up, and I felt safe. Maybe he even got me to laugh. In such a short time, I had made a new friend. He had taken good care of a scared young girl. He stayed with me until the shiny black and white car pulled up to the curb. And then I got my first (and only) ride in a squad car and turned to watch as my kind friend faded from view. I never saw him again.

Now, it was the job of my new friends in blue to get me home. It's a good thing that when my big brothers spent time with me, they taught me things like my full name and where I lived. (They also tried to get me to say "encyclopedia," and laughed as I tried and failed again and again.) I may have learned my home phone number as well; but even if I had, Mom and Dad and the rest of the gang wouldn't get home until after they had dropped off the

Bethel men at their dorms.

When they were able to reach him, Dad raced down to the police station to pick me up. I have no idea how hard it must have been for him to clear up this mess in the eyes of the law. His words must have shed ample light on things, for they did let him bring me home.

Years later, I asked two of my siblings if they knew what had gone wrong that day. My brother said that the older kids used to take turns being in charge of the young ones. He didn't know who was to be in charge of me that day, but in any event, no one saw that I was not in the car. So I think they all fell down on the job. My sister said that from then on, we had to do a head count every time we got in the car!

Our minds bury so many things that take place in the course of our long lives. This event from sixty years ago stays near the front of my thoughts. The fact that it was filled with pain and tears helps to keep it there. But the truth of how kind we can be to each other is just as strong as any of the fear. I am so glad to have spent time with the kind man whose name I do not know, and whom I will never see again.

44

A Happy Host

Becky Alexander

Travelers with wheeled bags rushed past me on their way to gates as an agent called out flight times. I had a full hour until my flight, so I slipped out of the stress and into a diner near my gate. A happy host found a booth for me and gave me a menu. Then he moved back to his spot by the glass front doors.

I could see the young man from my seat, and I couldn't help but watch him. He met guests with a bright smile and a quick wave. He hugged an aged woman. He rolled a man in a wheelchair through the crowd. He leaned down and shook the hand of a small boy.

When I was ready to leave, I walked up to the host and said, "You are so kind. I see how you treat guests. You spread lots of joy."

With his bright smile, he said, "The joy of the Lord is my strength!"

I knew the words of truth from Nehemiah 8:10 and said, "The joy of the Lord is my strength, too!"

I had been in awe of the way he was able to lift my heart, even though not near my table. He loved God, and that brought him inner joy. He didn't hold and hide that joy but shared it in caring ways with those who crossed his path.

Though I saw the young man only once, his bright smile often shines in my mind. And when the pace of my life gets too busy — much like an airport — I say, "The joy of the Lord is my strength."

45

Real Self Shining Through

by Pamela Groupe Groves

Our faces were pink from the sun and our smiles a tad worn out as we walked to Aunt Jackie's car after our once-a-year trip to the Canby Spring Yard and Garden Show. We filled her car trunk with our new garden tools and decor items. My ten-year-old daughter, Lisa, joined our new plants in the back seat, while I plopped into the front seat. Aunt Jackie drove on the quiet back road that wound to the freeway entry.

I gazed out the car window and soon felt as if I could nod off. But I roused in a flash when I saw a car coming straight at us. I had time for only two thoughts: *I am going to wake up in heaven or the hospital and Lisa is safe in the back seat.* I could feel my seatbelt pull tight on my body when the cars slammed into each other head on.

The next thing I saw was a man leap over the highway divider and rush to our car. When he came to my window and asked if we were okay I told him, "I think so." He ran to check on folks in the other car. Then he came back, "She is okay," he said. "But very upset because it's her son's new Mustang." He said she drove up the freeway's exit ramp thinking it was the on ramp.

Aunt Jackie began to feel dizzy and achy so he stayed next to her while we waited for the emergency crew that had been called. When the ambulance came, the man ran over to them to bring them to Jackie.

Once the man saw we were in safe hands, he turned to leave. I thanked him with a smile and in tears. He said he was glad to be there to help. Then, for the first time, I noticed his blonde hair worn in thick dreadlocks, the color-filled tattoos on his forearms, and his loose jeans. He did not fit my image of a man who would dash to a car wreck to give aid. I called out to him one last time, "Thank you!"

It has been years since the crash. The man's outer self might be the same, or he might have a new look. It is his kindness that brings him to mind, not his hair or tattoos. I am sure the real self he shared with us still shines from him. On that day he woke in my heart an urge to look at the real self in folks and ask, "Does the way I act show who I am?"

46

General Kindness

by Cristina Moore

A kind act by a stranger can change your whole life. It changed mine. I grew up in a small town in Tennessee after my mom, my sister, and I left Puerto Rico when I was five. Since 6th grade, after I watched films like the *Big Red One* and *Hamburger Hill*, I had dreamed of going to college at one of our nation's military schools so that one day that I could fight for my country.

From my first day in high school, I planned to apply to a military academy. I knew I had to raise my grades, to play sports, and to serve so I could be a strong applicant. The day came when I heard that three of the academies had accepted me. I chose West Point.

Each year, the Academy hosts Founder's Day meals where new cadets can meet others who have walked in their shoes. Even though I went to the meal, I didn't feel as if I fit in. I was in awe of those who had gone before me and felt meek when I viewed my deeds next to the feats of my peers. All about me were crisp uniforms, even those worn by the Color Guard as they staged the flags. I was dazed by all the events — the pomp and glitz. Yet, on that day, my mom had a quick chat with a stranger that would change the future for both of us.

The first year for a cadet at the Academy had none of that glitz. The cadet not only leaves friends and family behind but is thrown into a strict world full of order. It is fast paced. At the same time that the cadet gets books, garb, room, computers, and all she needs to study; she also has to run from place to place to learn how to march, to greet, and the other basics of military discipline. It was a first day of school like none of my friends back home faced in their colleges and one I hadn't seen in my mind's eye before I got there. Above all, I missed my home and my family. I felt alone, scared, and full of doubt. All I could think of was how I could make it one more day, let alone four more years. This was not like my dream; it was hard!

At the end of the day, I went back to my room to log on to my new computer. I was quite the sight with my hair in its new short trim and my shirt tucked into too-small shorts with white socks up to my knees. I did not feel like me. I saw that I had new mail in my box from the Dean. All I could think of was: *What did I mess up now?*

In the note, the Dean said that while I might not remember him, he remembered me. (He was right. I had no memory of a brief meeting on Founder's Day.) It turns out that on that day, he gave my mom his word that if I made it to West Point, he would look after me. He asked if he and his wife, Diane, could be my sponsors. It was signed, "Brigadier General Gerald E. Galloway, Dean of Academics."

I sat back in awe that this stranger had taken the time to write to me. That he asked me if I would have him as a sponsor. To a seventeen-year-old, this seemed very odd. Why would this man of high rank who didn't even know me take the time to offer his long-term help? A plain young girl from a small town in Tennessee, I was far from one of a kind.

Most of my friends did not have sponsors yet. Most of us didn't even know what sponsors did! All I could think of was what it would be like to have a place to rest away from school. So I said yes!

Through my years at West Point and after, he and his family played a key part in my job and my whole life. They gave me a home when I was far from mine. I would go to their house to eat, chat, and sleep on the floor while I watched TV. It was my home away from home.

In our senior year at school, we pick our military role. I chose engineer, the same as Brigadier General Galloway, from his impact on me as a cadet. He backed me up in school so I could push through the hard classes. He helped me to keep faith with my big dream so I would not let my doubts stop me from being the best I could be. Years later, he would call me — from a phone on a jet — on the day I took my first command. Last week, over twenty years later, he was with me virtually in this COVID world, while I bid adieu to my last command in the army as a brigade commander.

This kindness from a stranger so many years ago stirred me to offer my home to many soldiers and airmen through the years when they felt alone. We open our home the same way BG Galloway and his family shared their home and showed me that kindness. I hope that one day, one of them will look back, tell the tale of the kindness of a stranger, and choose to pass it on.

47

A "Chordial" Alto

by Karen O'Kelley Allen

As soon as I walked through the door of the church, my heart took on a life of its own as each beat got hard and fast. No doubt, it had been a bold move to come sing with a choir I did not know. But I wasn't sure it had been the right move until Donna spoke to me. Her words soothed my angst.

I had taken the seat next to her. While in a break, Donna told me her name and said she was glad I had come. Her crooked smile and warm eyes had made me feel more at ease.

The joy of Christmas was in the air and I yearned to join in the Christmas glee with its songs of cheer, but most of all I longed to share Christ's birth and peace to the world. So when I asked a good friend about her church and its choir, she had asked me to join. It's just that she couldn't be there that night.

But Donna didn't care that I had not joined the church and that I might not. She didn't even ask why I was there or why we had left our church or what our plans were. She just cared about me. Why should she? She didn't know me; yet I could tell that she cared. I came back the next week and the next. Donna would save a seat for me on the front row. The two of us would sing sure and strong. I could feel the pain from the loss of our old church start to melt. After a month, Donna and I learned our parts for each song and were set to go. The day came to sing in front of others, but my new choir friend had caught a cold of some sort. She did not show up to stand next to me to sing to the Lord. I was on my own. Her health was not the best, so she said, and she sensed it was time to take a step back in her life. She had made a hard-but-wise choice to let go of a choir that she had graced for many years.

Donna never came back. Her soft and kind words as well as her help to show me the ropes in choir that year struck a sweet chord in my heart that has never left. Ten years have passed. Her mind has since gone to a place that has no thought of right notes, cut-offs, or lead-ins. My husband and I joined the church that Christmas. Since then, I have sung more songs in that loft than I can count.

I am glad to have met Donna Dorsett. I am also glad I had a chance to tell her how much it meant to me that she reached out and made me feel at home that first day in choir. I can't help but think God used her for that brief span of time in my life to shine a light and bring back a spark of hope. I thank God for my brief but sweet time with a kind choir friend named Donna.

48

In No Man's Land

by Rich Kehoe

s dusk came, my wife and I and our six-month-old daughter were in California on an out-of-the-way route home from Oregon. About five miles back, we had passed a small town named Likely, population sixty-three. I joked with my wife that this would be a bad place to have the car break down. A few minutes down the road, our Honda Civic gave out, and the car came to a stop. My heart sank. What were we to do? We looked far and near for a house where we could get help, but found none. We couldn't call for help since in those days every phone was a landline. So, my wife picked up our baby, and we began to walk back to Likely, a town we weren't sure had even one gas station or a place to stay.

In no time, a stranger drove up and gave us a ride the rest of the way. He thought Likely could meet our needs. He took us to the only motel in town, which was in a state of ruin. It was next to a gas place that could also fix cars. But that was closed. The stranger told us to stay the night and check with the gas station the next day to get our car fixed.

The next day, we went to the gas station and told the man where our car was. He drove his tow truck to our car and checked it out. He said it had to have a new timing belt, but he didn't have the part in stock. He said he would tow our car to Susanville where he thought they would have the part. The tow cost would be two dollars per mile. So, with hope in our hearts, we hopped into the tow truck, baby and all, and he towed our car eighty-five miles to Susanville.

111

But even they did not have the part. I felt grim. Then, the tow-truck driver said he would tow us to Reno, Nevada, eighty-six miles more. He was sure they had the part there. What choice did we have? So, we got in the tow truck, and off we went.

In Reno, they did have the part and fixed the car in four hours. We tried to pay the tow-truck driver two dollars per mile, but he would not take it. He cut the bill in half and charged only one dollar per mile. In those days, this was still a large sum, but I felt less stressed by the bill than I would have.

As I think back on this time, I have faith that the stranger who gave us a ride and the stranger who towed us were used by God to help us and keep us safe. My trust grew when I saw that even in "no man's land" God has His eye on me to help in my time of need. *The Lord will watch over your coming and going both now and forevermore.*" (Psalm 121:8 NIV)

49

Umang's Taxi

by Leah Hinton

I was hit by a car. You heard me. I was hit by a car. Wait. Scratch that. Erase. Erase. That is not what went down. Let me start again. I was hit by a truck. A *truck*. A big black truck. (It is Texas, after all.) The year was 1997. I had bought a tuna on wheat for lunch and hit the knob on the metal pole to cross the street. My light turned green. I laughed at a joke told by the new girl from my work who was with me. Then, as I put one foot out and took a quick step to the side so as not to trip in a big pot-hole on the old Texas tar-top road, the truck hit me. Not straight on. Not so movie-like grand that I flew up in the air. But I was hit and hit hard. And, the side-step did me more good than to just save me from a hole. It kept me from being hit dead center and thus also kept me breathing.

I was even able to sit up while still in the cross-walk. My jeans had a tear at the calf. *That was a close one!* I thought. *I'll just get up and be on my way. Quick! Before the light turns.* Then it hit me. The truck had run the red light. I was angry. The truck ran the light. Did he not see me? He should have. Or he should have seen the light, at least. I still held my tuna on wheat in its clear take-out bag. I set it aside and put my palms down on the road and that's when I knew there was no way I was able to get up. Not on my own.

It is strange how pain can be slow. It's sort of like the way you can hear thunder long after you see light flash across the night sky. The pain came like thunder that is far away — a bit late to the party. By the time those few thoughts had pieced into a real idea as to how hurt I was, a man stood over me. He had black hair, brushed to cover a bald top. His shirt was old and worn but well kept. It seemed he took care of what he had but maybe didn't have much. His brow was wet with the sweat that the Houston heat soaks souls in every year, and we hadn't even hit the hot days yet. Still his smile was real and his teeth white against his dark skin. His English came hard. It rose up and down in a rhythm of lilts and beats, stops and starts — his voice a sort of music in my ears. And I was able to get what he said, yet I had a hard time with words of my own.

He was a lean man, not tall. Small even. He took my arm, heaved me up, and put me in the back of his taxi. No easy feat. I heard a voice say to wait for an ambulance. He said "NO" in a firm voice. He told the new girl from my work to get in so that I would not be alone. She said "no" and went back to her new job.

He drove me to the emergency room and spoke to me the whole way there. He noted that the cars were "heavy on the street" in Houston but that he knew a fast way. He told me how lucky I am to live in a city where I can go to a doctor so close. His father had been a doctor in India but in the United States worked at a gas station in Pasadena but was still happy to be in this country. His words over those few miles kept my mind busy as pain crept over my thoughts. I saw his name badge in the cab: *Umang*.

He may not have been my family by blood, but that day Umang was my family through deed. Later, I found out that he did not leave the hospital until he knew I was okay. He sat in a vinyl chair for hours while I had my jeans cut away and was sent for x-rays and a cat-scan of my brain since I had hit my head. My head was fine. But things from the waist down were not so great. I broke my knee cap and the two bones in my lower leg. I tore my cruciate ligament in half. My meniscus — on the inner side of the knee joint — was in shreds. Whew! And that was just what was wrong with my right leg. My left leg had quite a bit wrong with it as well.

A hospital is its own world where time can change pace at will. It runs slow for many things and goes blur-fast for others. Where I was, laid out flat on a bed with wheels, things were going quick. But where that lean man in white linen pants sat, things went at a snail's pace.

And the value of time can differ from one person to another. At any given time, it will have one level of worth to you and one level to me. In that hospital on that day, the value of time for a kind stranger who was there only to wait was very high. For Umang and his taxi-cab, time truly meant food and a home for him and who knows how many baby Umangs, and a Mrs. Umang as well. When I was his charge, he had no fares from his taxi-cab. He had no tips. He gave up all of that for me. Yet, had it not been for Umang, I would have been truly alone.

My husband was off-shore, at work as a Commercial Diver on an oil rig — hundreds of feet under water. My parents were in another city. I had lived in Houston for only two months. So at that point, the only one who even knew I was in the hospital was Umang.

This man saw to me. He picked me up off of the street, torn and hurt. Humbly, he stretched out his hand to give me the most costly thing he owned — his time — and with it all the help I could need. Thank you, Umang.

50

Good Samaritans

by Sharon Cook

Sharon, look!" My sister, Bonnie, poked at the sharp end of a nail in the side wall of her rear tire. We were on our way from her home in Fresno, California, to Kings Canyon National Park and had stopped at a store on the way. As she stepped out of the car, she looked down and saw the nail.

Kings Canyon National Park Visitor Center is at 6,500 feet; Fresno is 308 feet. What's more, the roads are not wide; they twist and turn. If she hadn't seen that nail, we could have been stuck on the side of one of those turns — miles from help or a tow truck. We are both in our 70s and do not know how to fix a tire. And, her three adult daughters who have Down Syndrome were with us. They can do many things but could not have helped us with a flat tire.

We drove to a tire store my sister uses. As we all walked from the car toward the store, two men came out to meet us. One worked at the store; the other was there to buy tires.

"Looks like you have a problem!" they both said at once.

"Yes," I said. "There's a nail in the rear tire, and we're on our way to Kings Canyon. Can it be fixed?"

"Hmmm, we're very backed up, but let me see what I can do." The man who worked there took the keys, pulled the car into the bay, and soon came back with the news. "You need a new tire. Because of where the nail is, this one can't be fixed. I'll squeeze you in right now." He looked at the other man. "He said you can have his spot in line. He'll wait to get his new tires put on."

It took only a short time to fix the tire. When it was done, Bonnie pulled out her charge card. Then the other man who came out to greet us stepped up and laid his charge card on the ledge.

"Put your card away. I'm paying for this."

She looked at him in shock. We didn't know him; he didn't know us. Why would he want to pay?

"Oh, thank you, thank you," my sister sobbed as she hugged the man and thanked him over and over. Bonnie is the only parent for these girls; she has to keep a tight rein on her funds so the one-hundred-dollar cost of the tire would have used money meant for other, more basic, needs.

Later the girls told us that the kind man's wife talked with them the whole time they sat there. One of the girls is less able than the others, and his wife spent the most time with her. She and her husband saw the need and stepped in.

We never knew their names and never saw them again. But thanks to their kind hearts, our day was safe; our trip didn't have to wait through a long delay; and my sister didn't even have to pay for the tire!

Only God

by Lin Daniels

Mom and I and I were on a drive of over 2000 miles from the East Coast to Oklahoma so I could start my new job as a gym teacher. Our first sight in the city was a billboard of a horse and a Ford truck with the words: "Ford, the next best thing!" In a state of culture shock, I asked myself, *Is it too late to turn back and go home?* To make things worse, once Mom left I would be all alone. I was scared to be so far from home where I didn't know even one soul.

At my new bank, a sweet lady named Bev set up my checking account. Her drawl was so thick that at times I couldn't quite grasp her words — but she seemed kind.

Two days later, I skipped church to buy a newspaper and scour its ads for a place to live. At the store, whom did I run into but Bev, along with her kids!

Bev said she would be happy to help Mom and me search for my new home. Should we agree to her offer? The folks I knew back East didn't often act like that. With two young kids in tow, she didn't seem a threat — though the thought that she could be an ax murderer did cross my mind!

Sometime after we first met, Bev told me that she had prayed for a good Christian friend to enter her life. As a young believer, I didn't even know you could ask God for stuff like that! Who would have guessed that a woman could reach out to be kind to someone she didn't know and end up with a lifelong friend? Only God!

The Eyes of a Stranger

by Beverly Varnado

I pulled into a space at the cafe, switched off the car, and sighed. I'd spent four weeks caring for my husband through his knee replacement. On this, his first day to drive again, he had plans. I was free to work on a book I'd begun months prior. That day, it was great just to drink coffee and write. I grabbed my purse and stepped from the car. But once out, I couldn't take a step. The next thing I knew, I fell head first into a curb.

At that point, all went white.

I rolled over, pulled up, and sat on the curb as a crowd formed. Dizzy, I tried to focus. The world seemed hazy. A hand reached out with a Kleenex, and I stared at it, not sure what to use it for.

"You need to wipe your face," said a voice from the fog.

I did, and red color soaked the paper in my hand.

Then a man I didn't know sat by me on the curb. "Hi," he said. "I'm an intensive-care nurse, and I'm here to help."

Here to help with what? I thought. More tissues appeared. Like a robot, I touched them to my face, and they soaked up even more of the red fluid.

"Call an ambulance," a voice said.

"No," I piped up. "I don't want to do that." *Why do I need an ambulance?* I glanced over and saw my cell phone on the ground. "I'll call my husband." When he answered, I said, "I fell at the cafe. Please come and get me," and hung up the phone.

A sick wave rose in me. "I need to lie down." I tried to reach for the car door, but my arm wouldn't work.

The nurse helped me lie in the back seat of the car. My body shook from what I later learned was shock.

"Call the ambulance," I heard the nurse say, and this time I didn't say no. He then climbed into the seat with me. "You've had a head injury," he said. "Don't go to sleep. Look at me." When he spoke in such a strong way, the very real chance that I might not make it dawned on me. I didn't want to end like that. I was ready, but I didn't want to leave my sweet family.

I stared into the eyes of this stranger whose gaze never left mine. When he hovered over me I thought about the way God leans over me with tender care. "Stay with me," he said. "Stay with me."

Despite my foggy brain, words from Psalm 46 came from my mouth: "God is our refuge and strength, an ever-present help in trouble. Therefore, we will not fear."

Hands cradled my head. Then I heard my husband's voice — edged in shock. "Oh, Bev," he said, when he first saw what a blood-soaked mess I was.

Soon, EMTs took over and moved me to the hospital. Once there, doctors warned us that I might have a serious head injury. But we were so blessed to hear that the tests showed only a concussion and fractured arm.

In the days after, I thought about that intensive-care nurse. I was sure that his Good Samaritan deed must have made him late for some event. But then I thought, *How alone I would have been if he had not helped me!* Until he showed up, I'd been offered only a tissue, and I'd been too dazed to know what to do with it.

Why I fell has been blocked out by the fall itself. But I will never forget what occurred after: that look in the eyes of a stranger and how he stayed with me.

If I ever see him again, I will be sure to thank him once more. And then I'll say, "My nurse friend, in many ways you were for me God's 'ever present help in trouble.'"

About the Authors

Jennifer Aaron (p. 81) followed her degree in English with a career as a stay-at-home mom. Now that her three daughters are adults, she can indulge her love of studying and writing about God's Word. Her devotions and stories have been published in *The Upper Room*, *devozine*, and several other magazines.

At her church, Jennifer mentors new Christians and leads the finance team. She loves to read, sew, and spend time with family and friends. She also tends to corner people so she can show them the latest pictures of her three amazing grandchildren, whom she visits as often as possible. Jennifer and her husband of 33 years live in western Washington, where he is a family physician.

Becky Alexander (p. 103) has three favorite words: adventure, ambition, and attitude. As a tour director, she leads tours to Washington DC, New York City, Toronto, Niagara Falls, and other destinations. Before her travel adventures, she served for 25 years as a children's minister.

Becky has been published over seventy times, including stories and articles in *Guideposts*, *Parent Life*, *Experiencing God*, *Special Education Today*, *The Minister's Family*, *Pockets*, *Christian Living in the Mature Years*, and *The Lutheran Digest*.

Born with one arm, Becky has worn a prosthetic arm since she was one year old. You can read about her experiences in *One Smile, One Arm* and online at www.onesmileonearm.com.

Karen O'Kelley Allen (p. 109) has a passion for music, ministry, and dogs. Retired from cancer research at the University of Alabama at Birmingham's O'Neal Comprehensive Cancer Center, she fills her time with lunch dates, writing, travel, family, exercise, and missions. She enjoys playing the organ for her church at Meadow Brook Baptist in Birmingham, Alabama where she and her husband of 38 years, George Parker (Parky), attend.

A diagnosis of breast cancer inspired her to write *Confronting Cancer with Faith* www.confrontingcancerwithfaith.com, a Bible study that has brought encouragement around the world. She has published numerous articles and devotionals through LifeWay Christian Resources, Grace Publishing, *The Alabama Baptist* newspaper, and other Christian magazines. Her blog http://ewerblessed.com/blog highlights everyday blessings, cancer blessings, and lessons from sheep.

Mary Alice Archer (p. 9) has worked in education for over 40 years. For the last 26 years she has taught middle schoolers math, English, history, French, art, drama, and science. Now she is tutoring Chinese students online.

She has a B.S. in Exceptional Education from the University of Central Florida and has written and illustrated the award-winning children's book, *If a Cat*. In addition, she has published in Focus on the Family's *Clubhouse Jr.* and in two previous editions of the *Short and Sweet* series.

A Southern California girl for the first 40 years of her life, she then moved to Central Florida. She and John have three children, six grandchildren, two Havanese dogs, a Bourke's parakeet, and a Hermann's tortoise named Melville, of course.

Janet Asbridge (p. 97) lives in cool, green southwest Washington state with her husband and her spoiled cat, Salty. When she's not writing; she enjoys reading, taking pictures, and creating mosaics.

Since her retirement as a reading specialist, she has had fun creating some early readers that can be found on Amazon.com. Her website, *Memory Hooks for Reading Books*, is designed to help families teach their young children to read without computer screens (memoryhooksforreadingbooks.net).

Adam Benson (p. 90) lives in Durham, North Carolina with his wife, Meghan, and their beagle, Charlie. Graduating from Furman University with a bachelor's degree in psychology and Duke Divinity School with a Master's in Divinity, he worked at Duke Law School. He has also worked as a youth minister. He is in the process of being ordained as an Elder in his Church agency and just received an appointment as co-pastor at 1st United Methodist Church in Elon, North Carolina.

He loved living and working in Yosemite National Park for two summers. He also loves to run, bike, write, play sports — golf and disc golf — and watch sports, movies, and TV shows on Netflix with his wife.

Nancy Brashear, Ph.D., (p. 52) has been writing since she was a child. As an adult, she has published short stories and poems. She won first place in the 2020 Casa Romantica Cultural Center and Gardens First Annual Poetry Contest, and her debut novel, *Gunnysack Hell*, is slated for publication in fall 2020.

Professor Emeritus from Azusa Pacific University, she has written articles and chapters for academic books and blog reviews for The International Literacy Association (for children's and adolescent literature). She met her husband when they were in the eighth grade, and she's the proud grandmother of seven talented and independent young girls (some already budding writers), ranging in age from four to twelve. Check her out at nancybrashear.com.

Susan Brehmer (p. 15), an encourager and Bible enthusiast, believes treasure is found in the Word of God and that time with Jesus sheds light on scripture. She loves to lead others into worship and through the life-changing Word of God. She has had fun crafting a ten-minute summary of the Old and New Testament as a souvenir of their journey together.

She thanks her violin students for opportunities to refine her motivational-speaking skills. She is grateful to friends and mentors who saw the writer in her before she made the discovery. She writes worship songs, devotional articles for the *Christian Journal* (thechristianjournal.org), devotions for *Pathways to God*, and can be reached at write2worship@gmail.com and profoundlysimple.net.

Beth Brubaker (p. 27) has been writing since her teens and a blogger and columnist since 2005. She is a humorist — focusing on clean family humor, children's stories, funny poetry, and songs. She is also a big fan of puzzle creation (both math and word puzzles) and is working on several books for publication.

Beth has been married to her Knight in Dented Armor since 1997 and has two children — a son with Asperger's and a horse-loving daughter, who provides most of the fodder for her humor writing. Her three cats — Scootch, Tinkerbelle, and Luna — provide the rest! She also has a fluffle of dust bunnies, a crash of dust rhinos, and a few dust elephants, because she's too busy writing to finish the housework.

Jenny Calvert (p. 39) and John, her husband of fifty years, have five children and twelve grandchildren. A lover of music, Jenny taught voice and piano and used her musical skills in churches for many years. This work and the duties of child-rearing caused her to put her love of writing on the back burner.

Now retired, her zeal for evangelism has led her down the path of writing Christian devotionals (including three devotionals published in *The Upper Room*). Jenny is also focusing on spiritual and Biblical growth.

Additional writing opportunities include being accepted as a contributing writer for www.dailyprayer.us under the link, "Daily Inspiration." She also writes a blog at www.libertyladiesdevotional.blogspot.com. Her piece in this book makes Jenny's fifth in the *Short and Sweet* series.

Frank Caudle (p. 34) pursued a B.A. in Theology and a M.A. in Education. Since then, oral communication has been part of his everyday life as he has taught both in the classroom and in the pulpit. He has also served as an Academic Dean in a Bible College where he taught the Life of Christ for 12 years.

Since that time, he has served different churches for 25 years. From the perspective of his broad background, he is now focusing on writing, speaking, and serving as a ministry consultant.

To fine tune his writing perspective, Frank belongs to Richmond Christians Who Write and a writers' critique group. He is also writing for a number of publications.

Ann L. Coker (p. 79) graduated from Asbury University 20 years after completing high school. After working as managing editor of *Good News* magazine, she contributed to *The Woman's Study Bible*. Currently she writes for devotional publications, other periodicals, and her blog (abcoker.blog). She has served the pro-life cause in several agencies.

Ann is married to her favorite preacher, Bill, now retired. Her current mission is to compile Bill's messages for publication, the first to be published in the fall of 2020. Her own book (unpublished) is a companion to John Bunyan's *The Pilgrim's Progress*. Ann is a member of Heartland Christian Writers in Indianapolis.

Ann and Bill have four children, ten grandchildren, and twelve great-grandchildren. Her hobbies include crafting cards and filling coloring books.

At an early age, **Patti Conn** (p. 95) discovered that she enjoyed reading, researching, and writing. She met her husband while attending Bethany Bible college near Santa Cruz, California. Partnering with her husband in ministry offered her diverse opportunities to use her writing skills, and she discovered that she also found joy in teaching.

Eventually, the couple and their son moved to Dallas, Texas, where for more than a decade she served as the managing editor at a ministry that produced a monthly magazine, books, newsletters, and other materials. Patti felt honored to serve in this challenging and fulfilling position. No matter where life has led, her love for writing never wanes. Recently retired, she continues to find great satisfaction in reading, researching, teaching and writing.

Dennis Conrad (p. 48) is a retired Professor of Speech Communications for Barstow Community College. While there, he also taught both speech and English for seven years at Fort Irwin, the National Training Center for the United States Army. In addition, Dennis and his wife, Diane, taught speech and English five summers in Kazakhstan, Central Asia, two summers in South Korea, and three summers in China.

By completing a one month, intensive writing program with the University of California, Riverside, he became a Fellow of the National Writing Project. He serves on the Board of Directors of Diamond Valley Writers' Guild in Hemet, California.

Dennis has been married to Diane for 30 years, and she is his editor.

Sharon Cook (p. 116) lives in Phoenix, Arizona. A retired teacher, she coordinates and leads Bible studies, gives talks on "Our Marvelous Brain," and presents history and destination lectures on cruise ships. She also loves to quilt for charity.

Widowed in 2016, Sharon spends summers in the White Mountains of eastern Arizona where, as a member of Arizona Volunteer Missions, she oversees the chapels at five RV parks. Her book, *Windows on the World, Lessons from Life*, is available on amazon. com. Visit her blog at: www.thetravelinglecturer.com.

Her husband's two children and their families live in California. Her son lives in Virginia and her daughter in Ohio with their families.

Lauren Craft (p. 71) enjoys writing about the abundant life that Christ promises (John 10:10) — one filled with purpose, joy, and lasting hope. Her devotions and stories have appeared in more than a dozen books, including three in the *Short and Sweet* series.

She also chairs her local Word Weavers chapter where every month her fellow writers inspire her. Lauren also aids in Bible translation, serves as a missions leader in her church, and shares her hope in Jesus in the U.S. and around the world.

God has blessed Lauren with a journalism post in downtown Washington, D.C., where she has been grateful to work for 12 years as a reporter and magazine editor. She lives in Woodbridge, Virginia. You can connect with her at laurenchristianauthor@gmail.com.

After 40 years, **Lin Daniels** (p. 118) retired from teaching physical education — all but one year in elementary-school. She and her twin sister are avid golfers. When playing as partners, they agree on which identical clothing to wear but choose one item (usually a hat) to be different.

Recently, Lin has found a passion for pickleball – a game similar to tennis but played on a smaller court while using a whiffle ball. Her other interests include writing Christian devotions, working with youth at church, and preaching on occasion. Lin gives thanks to God for the depths of His love as well as all the "surprises" He has graciously bestowed on her.

Karen Dorsey (p. 94) discovered a new passion when she joined Oregon Christian Writers twelve years ago to learn how to write. Since then, her published works have included articles in *LIVE* magazine, *Now What* online magazine, *The Upper Room, The Secret Place, Power for Living*, and in the book *Jesus Talked to Me Today*.

Above all, she is a teacher. Thirty-four years of elementary teaching and 41 years teaching every age from infants to 80-year-olds at church attest to this love. It's what fuels her writing, and it also came in handy when she was needed to homeschool two of her three grandsons during COVID-19. You can read more of her work on her blog www.karendorsey.me.

Steven Duke (p. 66) is retired from the US Air Force Reserve and Allstate Insurance Company. He now works part-time as an investigator for a large law firm.

He and his wife, Belinda, have four daughters and six grandchildren. Now that theirs is an empty nest, they have rescued two dogs — Barney and Piper — and a cat named Callie. Barney is Steve's shadow. Wherever Steve goes, Barney goes. Steve and Belinda are members of Wright Baptist Church in Fort Walton Beach, Florida. Steve also enjoys photography and playing disc golf.

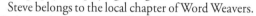

Steve belongs to the local chapter of Word Weavers. He has written three novellas, *Greg's Story*, *The Cleaner*, and *Ghost Ship*. He posts a chapter a day on Facebook at *Steven Duke Today*.

As the daughter of a career Army pilot, **Sharon Fincannon** (p. 67) traveled and moved several times in her childhood. In 2004 she married Mark Fincannon, a casting director in the film business. In the course of helping Mark on several film, television, and commercial projects, she's discipled several women in the film industry as well.

One of Sharon's own faith-filled experiences occurred in 2013 when she was diagnosed with breast cancer and miraculously healed. Many times she has seen God heal, redeem, and purpose her past pain for the good of others.

Sharon has two grown married daughters, Naomi and Heather, from a previous marriage. Mark also brought two daughters into their marriage, Christian and Mary. Between them, she and Mark have seven grandchildren.

Desiree Glass (p. 38) has written for numerous publications and websites including *Guideposts, Christian Devotions, A Joy-Full Season, Pen in Hand, Connections, Dragonfly, Element Connection, The Times-Crescent* newspaper, her church blog, and also two other books in the *Short and Sweet* series.

Desiree has 30 years of experience, teaching all ages from infant to adult. Currently she teaches high-school career-and-technology-education. She earned her B.S. at Salisbury University and her M.A. at Notre Dame of Maryland University.

Active in her church, she serves as trustee, greeter, and leader of a women's small group. She is the mother of three and grandmother of ten. In addition to spoiling the grandkids, she enjoys kayaking, hiking, and life on the farm. Her blog: http://desireeglass.blogspot.com.

Cynthia Conner Goyang (p. 31) and husband, Tony, have three adult sons and enjoy spending time with their three granddaughters. Born and raised in Denver, Colorado, and one of eleven children, she bears the scars of poverty softened and salved by the Balm of Gilead. As a Christ follower she seeks the answer for all worldly ills in God and God alone.

Cynthia is the author of *Just One Touch*, a Christian historical novel based on the woman with the issue of blood (Matthew 9:20-22; Mark 5:25-34; Luke 8:43-48). Her writing has also been published in *Guideposts* and *Angels on Earth*. Her Podcast, *For Such A Time As This*, is hosted on Apple Podcast, Spotify, and Google Podcast. She is a currently at work on *3Nights*, a fiction thriller.

Pam Groves' (p. 104) life has strayed a bit from the norm. After college she moved from Portland to teach school in an isolated rural town. She married fellow teacher, Stan, three months after they met. When their family grew to six adopted children, she chose a new role: stay-at-home mom.. Pam and Stan always took joy in their family and trusted that God was with them. At age 62, Stan passed away from a rare form of cancer.

Writing has been a part of her life since childhood. She considers writing for the Short and Sweet series a fun learning experience — building skills in choosing the best word and cutting what does not move the story forward. Read more about Pam at GrovesWords@gmail.com.

Based in Texas, **Leah Hinton** (p. 113) is a poet, short-story author, screenwriter, and playwright. Among her awards are the McClatchy Fiction Prize for her stories "Blue, Dark Fog," and "Spin-Me, Charlie"; the Poet's Prize for "Barefoot" (Dallas Area Writers), and the Audience-Choice Spotlight Award for her play, *Ripe* (2019 Stage Writers Festival).

Her play, *Paper Thin*, was a feature selection by Imprint Theatre in 2020. Her short films *Lost Man, Bantam,* and *Single* are in production for 2021 as part of the feature-length anthology, *Dad-Father-Papa*, from Carpe Diem Pictures. She is a full member of the Dramatists Guild, Associate Director of Stage Writers, President of the Writers Guild of Texas, Event Liaison of the DFW Writers Room, and founder of R.A.W. Arts Poetry Guild.

Becky Hofstad (p. 68) is an adoptive mother to two girls from Liberia: Naomi (age 12) and Tutu (age 8). Within six weeks of arriving in Minneapolis with new-parents Mike and Becky, Naomi saw snow for the first time and a medical device was surgically installed in her brain. Today, Naomi walks, downhill skis, and still cracks herself up when recording funny-face videos on her iPod.

Throughout their journey together, the family has experienced the kindness of many strangers, medical professionals, and teachers. Becky has taken writing classes at the Loft Literary Center and been recognized for her writing with a Minnesota Christian Writers Scholarship and awards from the Minnesota Christian Writers Guild and Faith Radio.

Award winning author, speaker, and blogger **Penny L. Hunt**'s (p. 42) writing has appeared in *Chicken Soup for The Soul, Guideposts, The Upper Room*, almost every edition of the *Short and Sweet* series, and on-line in *Just Eighteen Summers*. Her most recent book, *Bounce! Don't Break...* helps others bounce back from setbacks. *Little White Squirrel's Secret—A Special Place to Practice*, is an Amazon.com bestseller children's book dedicated to her severely autistic granddaughter.

Penny lives in the rural-peach-growing region of South Carolina with her husband Bill, a retired career naval officer and attaché, and their two dogs. While she enjoys gardening and gourmet cooking, her greatest passion is to lead others to a personal and intimate relationship with Christ. Visit her at PennyLHunt.com.

Tina M. Hunt (p. 61) is an ordained minister with the Church of the Brethren and an encouraging communicator, whether she's writing or speaking.

As her piece reflects, Tina is a 24/7 care giver for her mother in Arizona and long-distance wife to Nelson in Ohio. The apostle Paul penned the verse that has guided her life: "I want you woven into a tapestry of love, in touch with everything there is to know of God. Then you will have minds confident and at rest, focused on Christ, God's great mystery" (Col. 2:2, The Message Bible).

Her reflections and devotions appear on her blog, www.PotOfManna.wordpress.com, and also at www.almostanauthor.com. She loves to mine the nuggets of spiritual truth, using multisyllabic words only when necessary.

Deb Johnston (p. 33) writes about wetlands, birds, rivers, and Great Lakes — anything to do with nature. She is a retired educator living in central Wisconsin with her husband Stan, who is recovering at home after his surgery and 24-day hospital stay.

Her poem, "Oh Gentle Traveler," was recently featured in Poets to Come, a Poetry Anthology, and in May, 2019, she traveled to Long Island, New York, to present at a celebration of the Walt Whitman bicentennial. She has written for *The Mailbox, The Idea Magazine for Teachers.*

She is a member of the Wisconsin Fellowship of Poets, Society of Children Book Writers and Illustrators, and Wisconsin Wetlands Association. Find her on Twitter @johnstdeb and at dh-johnston.com.

Rich Kehoe (p. 111) came to Christ and was discipled by the Navigators. With his Master of Arts in theology from Talbot Theological Seminary and a passion to help people connect to God in a deep way, he has spent over 35 years serving in evangelical churches to disciple men and lead couples' groups in spiritual growth. He has also published a book titled Transforming Love – Growing in Intimacy with God and maintains a website and blog at http:journeyintolight.info that provides information and practical ways to further that intimacy.

Rich used his degree in Industrial Engineering and MBA in his career in administrative services for county government. Now retired and living in Highland, California, he and wife, Adele, have a daughter, a son, and three grandchildren.

Married for 41 years, **Liz Kimmel** (p. 100) has two children and four grandchildren. She earned a BA in Elementary Education at Bethel College in Arden Hills, Minnesota.

She has published two books of Christian prose/poetry and a grammar workbook for middle-school students. Her work has appeared in all books in the *Short and Sweet* series. Her devotions are included in the 2020 Guideposts book *All God's Creatures.* She is writing for several other Guideposts projects, including the new *One Minute Devotions.* She contributes puzzles to Focus on the Family's *Clubhouse Magazine.*

Liz is Communications Coordinator for her church. She writes and is the layout editor for a bi-monthly publication designed to inspire, strengthen, and edify readers.

Retired-registered-nurse **Janice Hagood LeMaster** (p. 44) and her husband, Bob, have three adult sons and four grandsons. Their weekly Sunday family dinners are lively and filled with fun. Janice and Bob enjoy traveling with her siblings and their families.

She and her sister, along with their husbands, have almost achieved their goal of traveling to all 50 states. They hope to travel to the remaining four states in the coming year. They particularly love trips on back roads with historical sites to explore.

When not travelling, Janice spends most of her time working in her home church and reading, writing, or researching her family history. She also loves attending Auburn University sporting events and any activities her grandsons participate in.

Dan Lewis (p. 75) is husband to Michelle, father to teenagers Nathan and Matthew, a youth minister, and a lover of God's Word. In 2015, he left his eighteen-year career as an electrical engineer to pursue student ministry. He also wanted to focus on time with his family — traveling and going on outdoor adventures, playing family games together, and serving together in the church and on mission trips as God calls them.

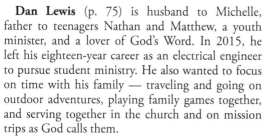

In February of 2020, 18-year-old Nathan was in a skateboarding accident that left him with a traumatic brain injury. Although Nathan remains in a minimally conscious state, the family has experienced the love and sustaining power of Jesus in powerful ways even in the midst of this difficult season.

Author and speaker **Terry Magness** (p. 13) is the founder of Grace Harbour Ministries, a biblically based teaching and discipleship ministry to the nations. Terry is passionate to help others know the character of God and who they are in Christ. She wants them to live victorious lives and grow to maturity in Christ, filled with His Spirit.

An ordained Assembly of God minister, her experience as a pastoral counselor and coach equips her to undergird and strengthen pastors and their wives, as well as credentialed women in ministry, and to encourage and empower the church.

Terry enjoys writing, photography, art, and fishing with her husband, Don. Their daughter Valarie, son Greg, daughter-in-law Jean Anne, and three granddaughters — Fallon, Savannah, and Kendall — keep them amazed, delighted, and ever thankful.

Donna Miesbach's (p. 18) inspirational poems and articles have spanned the globe for the past 35 years through publications such as Unity Magazine, Daily Word, Contemplative Journal, and Christian Living in the Mature Years. She is the author of the award-winning book, From Grief to Joy, A Journey Back to Life & Living. She is also the retired regional assistant to Coach Greg Roeszler, Founder & Executive Director of Playmakers Mentoring Foundation. In that role, Donna has co-authored all of Playmakers' Books.

In addition to her writing, Donna was certified as a meditation-and-yoga instructor through the Chopra Center for Well Being in California. She lives and works in Omaha Nebraska where she enjoys her children, grandchildren, and many great grandchildren.

Cristina Moore (p. 106) was born in Puerto Rico and grew up in Tennessee. She currently lives in North Carolina with her husband of over 20 years and her four children; Tripp, Katie, and twins Hope and Helena. She is the owner and CEO of Bronze Star Homes, an employee at Duke Energy, and and currently serves in the North Carolina National Guard as the Chief of the Joint Staff.

Cristina celebrates God's word by sharing the grace and miracles both she and her husband have witnessed through multiple combat deployments and their call to serve their community and country. Spending time with family is a priority and is enjoying returning to her passion of writing and touching the lives of those reading her work.

Donna Morse (p. 50) is a widow with three grown children, eight grandchildren, and five great-grandchildren and lives in Lacey, Washington. Donna is also a retired nurse and nursing instructor. Bible study for women is one of her passions and she teaches in her Abide Women's Bible Study group at church.

Her writing focus is interviews, devotionals, and short stories of various kinds. In her free time, she enjoys reading, writing, and watching movies at home or going to the cinema with friends. Getting out in nature to walk is a pleasure. Whether they're friends or family, Donna believes that people are delightfully special, so enjoying their fellowship over dinner or coffee, or just a good old fashion talk rates high on her priority list.

Alice H. Murray (p. 16) is an adoption attorney who has practiced law in Florida for over 30 years. She also serves as an officer and board member of the Florida Adoption Council and of Hope Global Initiative.

Alice's passion is writing. She is a staff writer for www.adoption.com and has been published in several books in the *Short And Sweet* series, in *Chicken Soup for the Soul*, and in the *Northwest Florida Literary Review*. Alice has written for legal-professional magazines, her local paper, a missions magazine, and various online sites. She particularly enjoys writing devotionals and sees teaching lessons everywhere.

In her spare time, Alice is a volunteer ESL (English as a Second Language) teacher for foreign-born residents in her area.

Suzanne Nichols (p. 63) grew up in Gulf Breeze, Florida where, during a high school composition class, she discovered the rewarding discipline of writing. Through the years, she has found creative expression in almost every genre of the printed word. She especially enjoys blending words and art in ways that can both delight and challenge the observer.

Suzanne is a charter member of her Word Weavers International chapter. She is published in six books of the *Short and Sweet* series and also a co-author of *COFFEE with God* and contributor to *Day by Day: 40 Devotionals for Writers & Creative Types*.

Suzanne lives in Hartselle, Alabama, with Roger, her husband of 44 years. They have three children and nine grandchildren who live much too far away.

Briana Novacek (p. 83) grew up in the country in southeastern Wisconsin in a tiny town called Byron. Living on an old farm gave her plenty of opportunities for exploration and the freedom to imagine. She moved to Eau Claire in 2009 to attend college, thinking she'd return home after getting her degree. But she fell in love with the Chippewa Valley. Today she and husband Matt live in Chippewa Falls, Wisconsin with their two young sons.

She is a stay-at-home mom, as well as a freelance book editor. She loves reading and writing stories about life that transcend the everyday. In her free time, she enjoys reading, going for walks, getting creative in the kitchen with new recipes, and spending time with family and friends.

In the foothills of the Great Smoky Mountains of East Tennessee, **Shelley Pierce** (22) and her husband, Tommy, raised their four children and now enjoy the gift of grandchildren. Tommy is the senior pastor of Towering Oaks Baptist Church and Shelley serves alongside him on staff as the director of preschool and children's ministries.

Shelley understands the challenges today's children face. She enjoys the friendships, laughter, and even the struggles of ministering in the lives of kids. Every experience presents an opportunity to learn more about God's great love.

Her publishing credits include T*he Upper Room* magazine; *Sweet Moments: Insight and Encouragement for the Pastor's Wife;* a middle-grade fiction series, *The Crumberry Chronicles;* and picture books, *I Know What Grandma Does While I'm Napping* and *High-Water Hattie.*

S.E. Pruitt is (p. 36) the oldest of six children, all of whom won the lottery by getting a set of parents who valued church, education, and cookies. She grew up in the San Francisco Bay Area and now lives in nearby Salinas. She is the fourth of five generations of teachers and taught middle school for about thirty years.

She wrote and privately published family histories and has a short story in the 2020 summer issue of *Woven Tales.* Since retirement, she has worked on three novels of historical fiction. She enjoys volunteering at her church, learning from her writing groups, having high tea with friends, and spoiling fourteen great-nephews and great-nieces, who all have a mad passion for gummy bears.

Reba Rhyne (p. 85), pen name of Reba Carolyn Rhyne Meiller, believes a writer should experience the setting of her work. So, she spends time in the territory she writes about — the western foothills of the Great Smoky Mountains —giving her stories the authentic quality readers crave. In her *Tipton Chronicles* series of five novels — *Butterfield Station, Chilhowee Legacy, My Cherokee Rose, Tipton's Sugar Cove-Matthew,* and *The Six at Chestnut Hill Farm* — Reba uses historical facts and places associated with her ancestors.

Reba retired as a consultant to the marine industry after prototyping upholstered interiors for major boat manufacturers from Texas to North Carolina. A Christ-follower for 60 years, she believes she should follow the Great Commission found in Matthew. She may be contacted at rebarhyne@gmail.com.

In the early 90s, **Valerie Runyan** (p. 29) submitted her first meditation to *The Upper Room*. It was not accepted; however, neither was it exactly a rejection. The editor encouraged her to submit again. That began her desire to send many more devotionals to this magazine — and several have been published with *The Upper Room*. Also as a result of that encouragement, Valerie has been published many times in *These Days*; and she wrote a month-long series in *Day by Day*.

She and her husband, Norman, celebrated 55 years together this year. He is a retired attorney, and their two favorite pastimes are walking and eating out. Valerie loves golf and has been playing for 42 years. She and Norman have two sons and six grown grandchildren.

Toni Armstrong Sample (p. 11) has served as a church elder, national speaker, retreat leader, Christian education leader, and women's group moderator. She contributed to the future direction on local boards of the American Red Cross, United Way, School Board Advisory Committee, and several businesses and as a workshop leader for the Manufacturer's Association of NW Pennsylvania and the National VA system.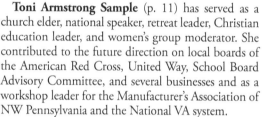

After retiring in 2000 from a career in human-resource management and consulting, Toni moved from Pennsylvania to South Carolina. Previously published in professional and recreational magazines and newspapers, she has since turned her writing into a powerful and passionate way of expressing her faith. She has published eleven novels, three autobiographical short-story books, and three devotional/Bible study books.

Xavia Arndt Sheffield (p. 46) has written music, lyrics, comedy spoofs, poetry, and Bible Studies — including *Life Principles from the Women of Acts*. She writes devotionals for *The Upper Room, These Days,* and the Washington National Cathedral. Her writing has appeared in *Monday Morning* and *Presbyterians Today* magazines.

A minister's wife of 40 years, she has been involved in most aspects of the church's life, including teaching Women of the Bible and other classes, creating Sunday School kickoff programs, acting as Children's Music Director, and creating over 1,000 bulletin boards (*Presbyterians Today,* March 2004). She holds a BA in music and an MA in speech/theater from SDSU. She and her husband have a daughter and a son.

Ann Clark Van Hine (p. 88) was born in Oxford, England but grew up in Oklahoma, Utah, Arizona, and New Jersey and now lives in Brooklyn. Ann is the mom of two daughters, the widow of a FDNY firefighter, a retired small-business owner, a docent with 9/11 Tribute Museum, a published writer, and a breast-cancer survivor.

Since September 11, 2001, Ann has travelled all over the USA and internationally in Ireland, Belgium, England, and Japan to share her story of God's presence and peace as she navigated "a personal loss in the midst of a national tragedy." She is currently seeking a publisher for her memoir. After many years of being Miss Ann at her studio and church, her favorite new title is "Mom-mom" to her three grandkids.

Beverly Varnado (p. 119) is a blogger and artist and also an award-winning author and screenwriter. Her Christmas novella, *A Season for Everything*, is slated for release in 2020 as a sequel to her novels *A Plan for Everything* and *The Key to Everything* — all set in the charming fictional town of Worthville, Georgia.

Her blog, *One Ringing Bell*, has nearly 1,000 posts in its archives. Her work has been featured on World Radio and in *The Upper Room* magazine and several other periodicals, anthologies, and online sites. Having recently exhibited in a state-university gallery, she is always working on a new painting. She lives in North Georgia with her husband, Jerry, and is Mom to three and Mimi to two. Learn more at www. Beverly Varnado.com.

Wilma Vernich (p. 24) writes from the perspective of a mother of two and a farmer's daughter. Learning on the knee of her father and through Scrabble games with family, Wilma went on to study journalism in college — infatuated with the power of prose. Although she has not written her book yet, Wilma often expresses her innermost yearnings through poetry and her desire to encourage people through her meditations for *The Upper Room*.

In addition to baking homemade bread, Wilma can claim the old-fashioned love of writing letters and sending them through "snail mail." She lives outside Nashville, Tennessee where she can see pretty sunsets and loves to be outside — whether it's working in the yard, waterskiing on a lake, or riding her bike.

Alyssa Wedemeyer (p. 73) is a 24-year-old expectant mother with an extensive background in Christian leadership. She currently attends Liberty University Online based in Lynchburg, Virginia, to earn her Bachelor of Science in Religion with a focus on apologetics. Her passions include writing, speaking, and mentoring young women in her community based in Vancouver, Washington.

When not speaking or writing, she can be found reading books, cuddling with her mini-Australian shepherd, Luka, playing board games with her family, or having conversations with her husband, Keli'i.

Alyssa's work has been in *Short and Sweet's Humiliating Tales We Wish wWeren't True* and in *Brio* magazine. She feels called to encourage and inspire young female believers to become disciples of Christ, standing firm in their faith above everything else.

Kenneth Avon White (p. 19) lives in Gastonia, North Carolina where he works to equip employees to successfully adjust to workplace changes. But in Ken's other world, change is welcome. Plots and characters and settings all adjust to an ever-changing landscape as stories unfold like a yellow brick road that leads to someplace magical.

Ken's devotionals have been published in *The Upper Room* magazine, and other short pieces in several books in the *Short and Sweet* series. In a time of adjusting to a "new normal" brought on by COVID-19, Ken is finally outfitting the home he bought in the summer of 2019. Two other things are top-of-mind for Ken — finding ways to help others during this pandemic and finally writing his first novel.

Karen Woodard (p. 92) lives in North Carolina where she enjoys spending time with her husband and family, which now includes five children, two sons-in-law and one grandchild. Her favorite activities are reading, crocheting, spending time outdoors, and writing Christian poetry and devotions. Some of her writings have been published in *The Upper Room* devotional magazine as well as in *Short and Sweet Goes Fourth* and *Short and Sweet's Family Album*.

Her inspiration for this writing was the kindness shown to her family through a stranger during the difficult days following her son's traumatic brain injury in 2014. That experience gave her insight into the importance and healing power a kind act can hold for others.